HOW TO FORM A
LIMITED LIABILITY COMPANY

by
Margaret C. Jasper

Oceana's Legal Almanac Series:
Law for the Layperson

Oceana®
NEW YORK

OXFORD
UNIVERSITY PRESS

Oxford University Press, Inc., publishes works that further Oxford University's objective of excellence in research, scholarship, and education.

Copyright © 2007 by Oxford University Press, Inc.
Published by Oxford University Press, Inc.
198 Madison Avenue, New York, New York 10016

Oxford is a registered trademark of Oxford University Press
Oceana is a registered trademark of Oxford University Press, Inc.

Library of Congress Cataloging-in-Publication Data

Jasper, Margaret C.
How to form a limited liability company / by Margaret C. Jasper.
    p. cm. -- (Oceana's legal almanac series: law for the layperson)
Includes bibliographical references.
ISBN 978-0-19-533901-7 ((clothbound) : alk. paper) 1. Private companies--United States--Popular works. 2. Limited partnership--United States--Popular works. I. Title.
KF1380.Z9J37 2007
346.73'0668--dc22

2007029897

Note to Readers:

This publication is designed to provide accurate and authoritative information in regard to the subject matter covered. It is based upon sources believed to be accurate and reliable and is intended to be current as of the time it was written. It is sold with the understanding that the publisher is not engaged in rendering legal, accounting, or other professional services. If legal advice or other expert assistance is required, the services of a competent professional person should be sought. Also, to confirm that the information has not been affected or changed by recent developments, traditional legal research techniques should be used, including checking primary sources where appropriate.

(Based on the Declaration of Principles jointly adopted by a Committee of the American Bar Association and a Committee of Publishers and Associations.)

To My Husband Chris

Your love and support
are my motivation and inspiration

To My Sons, Michael, Nick and Chris

-and-

In memory of my son, Jimmy

Table of Contents

CHAPTER 9:
TAXATION ISSUES

How to Form a Limited Liability Company

ABOUT THE AUTHOR

MARGARET C. JASPER is an attorney engaged in the general practice of law in South Salem, New York, concentrating in the areas of personal injury and entertainment law. Ms. Jasper holds a Juris Doctor degree from Pace University School of Law, White Plains, New York, is a member of the New York and Connecticut bars, and is certified to practice before the United States District Courts for the Southern and Eastern Districts of New York, the United States Court of Appeals for the Second Circuit, and the United States Supreme Court.

Ms. Jasper has been appointed to the law guardian panel for the Family Court of the State of New York, is a member of a number of professional organizations and associations, and is a New York State licensed real estate broker operating as Jasper Real Estate, in South Salem, New York.

Margaret Jasper maintains a website at http://www.JasperLawOffice. com.

In 2004, Ms. Jasper successfully argued a case before the New York Court of Appeals, which gives mothers of babies who are stillborn due to medical negligence the right to bring a legal action and recover emotional distress damages. This successful appeal overturned a 26-year old New York case precedent, which previously prevented mothers of stillborn babies to sue their negligent medical providers.

Ms. Jasper is the author and general editor of the following legal almanacs:

AIDS Law
The Americans with Disabilities Act
Animal Rights Law
Auto Leasing
Bankruptcy Law for the Individual Debtor
Banks and their Customers
Becoming a Citizen
Buying and Selling Your Home

Commercial Law
Consumer Rights and the Law
Co-ops and Condominiums: Your Rights and Obligations As Owner
Copyright Law
Credit Cards and the Law
Custodial Rights
Dealing with Debt
Dictionary of Selected Legal Terms
Drunk Driving Law
DWI, DUI and the Law
Education Law
Elder Law
Employee Rights in the Workplace
Employment Discrimination Under Title VII
Environmental Law
Estate Planning
Everyday Legal Forms
Executors and Personal Representatives:
Rights and Responsibilities
Harassment in the Workplace
Health Care and Your Rights
Health Care Directives
Hiring Household Help and Contractors: Your Rights and Obligations
Under the Law
Home Mortgage Law Primer
Hospital Liability Law
How To Change Your Name
How To Form an LLC
How To Protect Your Challenged Child
How To Start Your Own Business
Identity Theft and How To Protect Yourself
Individual Bankruptcy and Restructuring
Injured on the Job: Employee Rights, Worker's Compensation and
Disability Insurance Law
International Adoption
Juvénile Justice and Children's Law
Labor Law
Landlord-Tenant Law
Law for the Small Business Owner
The Law of Attachment and Garnishment
The Law of Buying and Selling
The Law of Capital Punishment
The Law of Child Custody
The Law of Contracts

The Law of Debt Collection
The Law of Dispute Resolution
The Law of Immigration
The Law of Libel and Slander
The Law of Medical Malpractice
The Law of No-Fault Insurance
The Law of Obscenity and Pornography
The Law of Personal Injury
The Law of Premises Liability
The Law of Product Liability
The Law of Speech and the First Amendment
Lemon Laws
Living Together: Practical Legal Issues
Marriage and Divorce
Missing and Exploited Children: How to Protect Your Child
Motor Vehicle Law
Nursing Home Negligence
Patent Law
Pet Law
Prescription Drugs
Privacy and the Internet: Your Rights and Expectations Under the Law
Probate Law
Protecting Your Business: Disaster Preparation and the Law
Real Estate Law for the Homeowner and Broker
Religion and the Law
Retirement Planning
The Right to Die
Rights of Single Parents
Small Claims Court
Social Security Law
Special Education Law
Teenagers and Substance Abuse
Trademark Law
Trouble Next Door: What to do With Your Neighbor
Victim's Rights Law
Violence Against Women
Welfare: Your Rights and the Law
What if It Happened to You: Violent Crimes and Victims' Rights
What if the Product Doesn't Work: Warranties & Guarantees
Workers' Compensation Law
Your Child's Legal Rights: An Overview
Your Rights in a Class Action Suit
Your Rights as a Tenant

Your Rights Under the Family and Medical Leave Act
You've Been Fired: Your Rights and Remedies

INTRODUCTION

The Limited Liability Company, commonly referred to as an LLC, has become a popular organizational structure for small businesses that want to combine the limited liability advantage of incorporation with the pass-through taxation feature of the sole proprietorship or partnership.

This almanac examines the nature of the LLC and sets forth the basic requirements for setting up an LLC, which includes naming your business, completing your LLC Articles of Organization, filing your paperwork and paying your fees. This almanac also discusses the creation of an LLC operating agreement, a document which contains the financial and managerial rights and responsibilities of the members of the LLC, including capitalization, allocation of losses, distribution of profits, and dissolution of the LLC.

This almanac explains the process of converting an existing business into an LLC, the formation of a professional limited liability company, and the ability of a foreign LLC—out-of-state or country—to do business in a particular state.

The Appendix provides sample documents, resource directories, and other pertinent information and data. The Glossary contains definitions of many of the basic legal terms used throughout the almanac.

CHAPTER 1:
CHOOSING A BUSINESS STRUCTURE

IN GENERAL

It is important to understand the various types of business structures available before you settle on the limited liability company (LLC) to ensure you have chosen the best form of business ownership to meet your needs. The LLC is a fairly recent type of business structure. Prior to the advent of the LLC, there were three basic types of business structures most commonly used by small businesses: (1) the sole proprietorship; (2) the partnership; and (3) the corporation.

The type of business you form will affect the way in which you must operate your business, therefore, you should consider the restrictions and limitations of each before making your decision. Your choice will have long-term implications, so you are advised to consult with an accountant and/or attorney in making this choice.

No matter what business structure you choose, if your needs change, you can change the structure of your business. For example, if you start out as a sole proprietorship, but need additional funding, or someone who can contribute additional management skills, you may want to bring in a partner.

Some factors you should take into consideration include:

1. The nature of your business.

2. The size of your business.

3. The amount of control you want to maintain over the business.

4. The type and extent of liability you are willing to risk.

5. The tax implications.

6. The anticipated profits of the business.

7. The liquidity of the business should you wish to end the business.

Following is an overview of the pros and cons of the various types of business structures available to the prospective business owner.

THE SOLE PROPRIETORSHIP

The sole proprietorship is the simplest and most common business organization, and the least expensive of the three basic forms of doing business. It is simple and inexpensive to start, and easy to dissolve. The sole proprietorship is owned and operated by one person—the sole proprietor—and continues until his or her death or retirement.

The sole proprietorship may be operated in the individual owner's personal name, or under an assumed business name, also known as a "DBA"—e.g., John Smith d/b/a Smith's Hardware Shop. The sole proprietor runs the day-to-day operation of the business and exercises total control over the business. The sole proprietor owns all of the assets of the business and income generated by the business.

Unfortunately, there are drawbacks with this type of business formation. The sole proprietorship does not afford the owner any protection from the debts and liabilities of the business. The sole proprietor has unlimited liability, which places the owner's business as well as personal assets at risk. For example, if the business incurs a debt, the business creditor can go after the owner's personal assets to recover the debt. The sole proprietor is also personally liable for all of his or her own acts, as well as all acts of employees committed within the scope of their employment.

The sole proprietorship itself does not pay any taxes thus there is no need to file a separate business tax return. The sole proprietor retains the profits of the business. The income and expenses from the business are shown on IRS Schedule C, which is made part of the business owner's personal income tax returns. If Schedule C shows that the business earned a profit, that amount is added to all other income the individual earned that year from whatever source. On the other hand, if the business shows a loss, that amount is deducted, thereby reducing the total income subject to taxation. However, whether or not the business has a loss, a sole proprietor is required to pay self-employment tax for social security coverage.

THE PARTNERSHIP

A partnership is formed when two or more persons agree to start a business, each generally making a contribution to the venture, such as money, property or services, with the intention of sharing the profits and losses from the business. Since a corporation is a legal person, it may be a member of a partnership if such membership is in furtherance of the corporation's purpose. The partnership name may consist of the names of the partners or, as with a sole proprietorship, the partnership name may be an assumed name. Partners are liable for their own acts, as well as the acts of the other partners.

The partners generally enter into a written partnership agreement that spells out all of the rights and responsibilities of each partner. A partnership may also arise out of an oral agreement, although such an agreement would be difficult to prove, thus a written partnership agreement is always recommended.

A well-drafted partnership agreement should include the following:

1. Type of business.

2. Amount of equity invested by each partner.

3. Division of profit or loss.

4. Partners' compensation.

5. Distribution of assets on dissolution.

6. Duration of partnership.

7. Provisions for changes or dissolving the partnership.

8. Dispute settlement clause.

9. Restrictions of authority and expenditures.

Although a partnership does not pay any tax, it must file an information return setting forth the profits and losses of the partnership. The profits and losses of the partnership flow through to the individual partners. The individual partners must report their shares of the partnership profits or losses on their personal income taxes, in much the same manner as the sole proprietor. Unless the partnership agreement provides otherwise, partners generally share profits equally, and share losses in the same proportion as profits. In addition, each partner is also required to pay self-employment tax for social security coverage.

General and Limited Partnerships

The two basic types of partnerships are the general partnership and the limited partnership. In a general partnership, all of the partners, known as general partners, share fully in the profits, losses and management of the company. In addition, each partner has unlimited personal liability.

A limited partnership consists of one or more general partners, who manage the business and are personally liable for partnership debts, and one or more limited partners, who contribute capital and share in profits, but take no part in running the business and are not liable for the debts of the partnership beyond their capital contributions.

The advantage of a limited partnership over a general partnership is the limited liability afforded the limited partners, as long as the limited partner does not take an active role in managing the business.

The Limited Liability Partnership (LLP)

Like a limited liability company, the limited liability partnership (LLP) is relatively new type of business formation that combines elements of a partnership and a corporation. In an LLP, all of the partners have a form of limited liability like the shareholders of a corporation and the members of an LLC, however, the partners have the right to manage the business directly, and the LLP is taxed differently from the corporation. In addition, limited liability partnerships are distinct from limited partnerships in that limited liability is granted to all partners, not only to a certain sub-group of "limited partners" who are not involved in managing the partnership. Thus, the LLP is especially favorable when all of the investors in the partnership want to take an active role in managing the business.

The limited liability partnership is discussed more fully in Chapter 3 of this almanac.

THE CORPORATION

A corporation is a legal entity, separate from its owner, created under the authority of the laws of the state in which it conducts business. This is true even if all of the shares in the corporation are owned by only one person. Control depends on stock ownership. Persons with the largest stock ownership, not the total number of shareholders, control the corporation. With control of stock shares—i.e., 51 percent of the corporation's stock—a person or group is able to make policy decisions. Control is exercised through regular board of directors' meetings and annual stockholders' meetings. Records must be kept to document decisions made by the board of directors. Small, closely held corporations can operate more informally, but recordkeeping cannot be eliminated entirely.

Business corporations are either public or private. A public business corporation refers to one that trades its shares to and among the general public, as opposed to a private business corporation, also known as a close corporation, whose shares are not publicly traded.

Incorporation has some advantages over the sole proprietorship and partnership forms of doing business. For example, incorporation may provide limited liability for the shareholders. Thus, if the corporation enters into a contract for the purchase of goods, and it breaches the contract and does not pay for those goods, the creditor can only enforce a judgment against the assets of the corporation. The assets of the shareholders and officers cannot be touched unless the creditor "pierces the corporate veil."

If the shareholders do not operate the corporation as a separate and distinct entity, with all the legal formalities, a court may conclude that the business is not a true corporate entity and the court may "pierce the corporate veil." When this happens, personal liability may be imposed on the shareholders. This could occur, for example, where the shareholders commingle corporate and personal funds or do not maintain the proper corporate records. Further, officers of a corporation may be liable to stockholders for improper actions.

In addition, particularly in states where corporations are required to maintain a minimum amount of capital as a condition of doing business, courts will pierce the corporate veil if they determine that the corporation is not adequately capitalized.

There are some exceptions to the limited liability feature of incorporation. For example, creditors of closely held corporations will likely require a personal guarantee from one or more of the shareholders or officers before extending credit to the corporation. The person who gives that guarantee will be personally liable for that particular corporate debt should the corporation fail to pay.

There are three basic types of corporations:

The C Corporation

The standard corporation—known as a C corporation—unlike a sole proprietorship or partnership, files a corporate tax return that shows the corporation's income, which is subject to taxation. Income received by the owner of the corporation, as a shareholder/employee, which may be in the form of a salary, dividend, or interest income, is taxable to the individual and reported on his or her personal income tax returns. When the corporation pays out salaries or interest, just as any other corporate expenses, these items are generally deductible. On the other hand, dividends are subject to corporate tax, as well as taxable to the stockholder on his or her personal income tax returns, resulting in a double taxation of the same funds.

The Subchapter S Corporation

In order to avoid the double tax discussed above, some corporations elect, for tax purposes, what is known as "S" corporation status under Subchapter S, Section 1362 of the Internal Revenue Code. An S corporation files an information return instead of a regular corporate return, and does not pay taxes on the income of the corporation. The corporate income and losses are passed through, on a pro-rata basis, to the shareholders, who report their shares of the income or losses on their personal income tax returns, much like a partnership.

In order to elect S corporation status, the corporation must meet certain statutory requirements. For example, among other requirements, an S corporation must be a domestic corporation that is not a member of an affiliated group of corporations; it cannot have more than a certain number of shareholders (a husband and wife may be counted as one shareholder); and the shareholders must be individuals, estates, or certain trusts, and cannot be nonresident aliens. In addition, there can only be one class of stock.

Once S corporation status is elected, it continues until revoked. Therefore, you can maintain an S corporation as long as this arrangement benefits you, assuming you continue to meet the statutory requirements.

The Professional Corporation

In most states, professionals—such as accountants, doctors, lawyers, and dentists—are permitted to form a corporation. Shareholders must be duly licensed in the profession. Many professional corporations are formed to allow the shareholders to take advantage of the tax benefits of incorporation. The shareholders of a professional corporation also enjoy limited liability for all claims except in the case of professional malpractice. If a shareholder commits an act of professional malpractice, he or she is personally liable.

CHAPTER 2:
THE LIMITED LIABILITY COMPANY (LLC)

WHAT IS A LIMITED LIABILITY COMPANY?

The Limited Liability Company (LLC) is a fairly new form of business structure available in all fifty states which has become a popular choice among business owners since its creation. The LLC is a hybrid business formation with certain advantageous features of both a partnership and a corporation. The LLC only requires one owner—known as a member—to form the business. A member may be an individual, a corporation, a partnership, another limited liability company, or any other legal entity.

WHAT IS A PROFESSIONAL LIMITED LIABILITY COMPANY

One or more professionals may form a Professional Limited Liability Company (PLLC). A PLLC is formed for profit for the purpose of rendering the professional services of the members of the PLLC. For the purposes of the PLLC, the term "profession" generally includes acupuncture, architecture, athletic training, audiology, certified shorthand reporting, chiropractic, dentistry, dietetics and nutrition, engineering, interior design, land surveying, landscape architecture, law, massage therapy, medical physics, medicine, midwifery, nursing, occupational therapy, ophthalmic dispensing, optometry, pharmacy, physical therapy, podiatry, psychology, public accountancy, respiratory therapy, social work, speech-language pathology and veterinary medicine.

ADVANTAGES OF THE LLC

Many business owners are choosing to form a limited liability corporation because it offers a number of advantages over other business structures, as set forth below.

Pass Through Income

For tax purposes, the LLC is treated like a partnership. The profits and losses of the business are passed through—i.e., distributed—to the owners and investors, and reported on their personal income tax returns.

LLC tax issues are discussed more fully in Chapter 9 of this almanac.

Limited Liability Feature

The LLC has the limited personal liability feature of the corporation; thus, the LLC members are not responsible for business debts or claims. This is particularly attractive for the small business owner, who may be concerned about the unlimited liability of a sole proprietorship. In fact, this threat of personal exposure deters many potential entrepreneurs from starting new businesses.

For example, if the business is sued by a person injured on the business premises, and the injured person obtains a money judgment, the judgment cannot be enforced against an LLC member. The injured person—known as the judgment creditor—cannot go after the LLC member's personal assets, home, etc. This is so even if the business is unable to pay the judgment.

It should be noted, however, that limited personal liability is not absolute under certain circumstances. For example, if the LLC member personally guarantees a business debt, the creditor could hold the individual responsible if the creditor cannot collect from the business. In addition, if the LLC member causes direct harm or injury to another, or to the business, he or she would be responsible for damages.

For example, if the LLC is a hair salon owned by a hairdresser, and the hairdresser accidentally scalds a client with boiling water, the LLC owner—the hairdresser—would be personally liable to the injured client despite the limited liability feature of the LLC.

Further, if the LLC member runs the business informally as a sole proprietorship, instead of a separate business entity, he or she may be held liable for business debts.

For these reasons, it is advisable to consult your insurance representative regarding a liability insurance policy for your business to cover you against losses that are not subject to the limited liability provisions of the LLC.

Flexibility

Although the S corporation operates in much the same way as an LLC—i.e., it limits personal liability and is taxed like a partnership—the S corporation is much more complex and subject to many more restrictions than the LLC. For example, whereas the S corporation limits membership to individuals, estates and certain trusts, which can total no more than 35, the LLC is more flexible, allowing corporations, partnerships, charitable organizations, pension plans, nonresident aliens and other trusts to participate. In addition, the LLC may offer more than just one class of stock, unlike the S corporation.

The LLC also has advantages over the regular corporation and the limited partnership, both of which have drawbacks. As discussed above, the regular corporation involves double taxation of dividend income and there are a number of formalities that must be followed to maintain corporate status whereas the LLC is not required to observe corporate formalities. The limited partnership runs the risk of reclassification as a general partnership if the limited partner is determined to have taken an active part in managing the business whereas all of the members of the LLC (and partners in the LLP) can be actively involved in the company's operations.

DISADVANTAGES OF THE LLC

The LLC is not right for every business owner. Formation is more complex and formal than that of a general partnership. In addition, an LLC is dissolved when a member dies or files bankruptcy, unlike a corporation, which continues to exist.

Further, the LLC restricts the transferability of company interests, whereas the corporation allows unrestricted transfer. Thus, if your business will require the right to transfer interests without restriction, the LLC is not the right choice.

In any event, since laws concerning the LLC vary from state to state, until a uniform LLC law is adopted by all jurisdictions, it is imperative that you thoroughly investigate the LLC regulations for the state in which you intend to do business before deciding on using this form of organization.

FORMATION REQUIREMENTS

LLC formation basically involves four main steps: (1) naming your company; (2) filing articles of organization; (3) creating an operating agreement; and (4) obtaining any required license and permits.

Step One: Name Your Company

There are certain requirements that must be followed when naming your company. For example, the name you choose cannot be the same as the name of another limited liability company. In addition, the name must include some word or abbreviation that designates the company as an LLC, e.g., "Mary's Bake Shop, a Limited Liability Company."

The requirements for naming your company are set forth more fully in Chapter 4 of this almanac.

Step Two: File Articles of Organization

Your LLC's articles of organization—also referred to as a certificate of formation in some jurisdictions—must be filed with your state's Secretary of State along with the required filing fee. The articles of organization generally set forth basic information about the LLC, such as its name, address, registered agent, members, etc.

LLC Articles of Organization are discussed more fully in Chapter 5 of this almanac.

Step Three: Draft an Operating Agreement

Depending on your state, you may need to create an operating agreement. An operating agreement is similar to a partnership agreement or corporate by-laws. The operating agreement sets forth rules by which your LLC will function, e.g., the members rights and responsibilities, company management, profit sharing, etc. It is advisable for you to draft an operating agreement for your LLC whether or not your state requires one.

The LLC operating agreement is discussed more fully in Chapter 6 of this almanac.

The reader is advised to check the law of his or her jurisdiction for state-specific regulations. For example, some states require publication of a notice in the newspaper stating the owner's intent to form an LLC.

Step Four: Obtain License and Permits

Your state may require you to obtain certain licenses and permits in order to begin doing business, such as a business license.

License and permits are discussed more fully in Chapter 8 of this almanac.

CONVERTING AN EXISTING BUSINESS TO AN LLC

You are not obligated to maintain a certain type of business structure. If your needs change, you can always convert a sole proprietorship or partnership to an LLC. The process may be as simple as filing a form with the Secretary of State. Some states may have additional requirements, therefore the reader is advised to check the law of his or her jurisdiction for specific instructions.

A sample Certificate of Conversion is set forth at Appendix 1.

DOING BUSINESS OUT-OF-STATE

An LLC is only considered a domestic business in the state of it's formation. For example, if you formed your LLC in New Jersey, it is only considered a domestic LLC in New Jersey. If you transact business in states other than New Jersey, you are required to "foreign qualify" your LLC in those states before you can transact business. In general, you must apply for a certificate of authority, and pay any required fees, in the state where you intend to do business. This gives the new state notice that a foreign LLC is doing business within the state.

Before a state will approve your application for a certificate of authority, it will require submission of a certificate of good standing from the state in which you formed your LLC. If your LLC is not "in good standing," in the state of formation, e.g., because you failed to pay your franchise taxes, it is unlikely you will be given a certificate of authority to do business in the new state. Your application for a certificate of authority, the certificate of good standing, and the required filing fees must be filed with the appropriate state agency.

A sample application for a certificate of authority is set forth at Appendix 2.

If you fail to qualify as a foreign LLC in a state in which you are transacting business, you forfeit certain rights. For example, your LLC would not have the right of access to the state's courts, if necessary. Therefore, you could not bring a lawsuit in the state, nor could you defend a lawsuit if your LLC was sued. In addition, your LLC would be subject to fines, penalties, and back taxes.

The following criteria generally determines whether you need to qualify your LLC in another state:

(1) Whether the LLC has a physical presence in the state;

(2) Whether the LLC has employees in the state;

(3) Whether the LLC accepts orders in the state; and/or

(4) Whether the LLC has a bank account in the state

If you do not want to qualify as a foreign LLC in another state, you can register your LLC as a domestic LLC in that state. One advantage of forming a new LLC in each state in which you intend to do business is the separation of liabilities. For example, if one of your LLCs goes bankrupt in one state, the assets of the LLC in another state could not be used to pay the debts of the LLC that went bankrupt.

CHAPTER 3:
THE LIMITED LIABILITY PARTNERSHIP
(LLP)

DEVELOPMENT OF THE LIMITED LIABILITY PARTNERSHIP

A number of years ago, professionals, such as lawyers and doctors, were not allowed to form corporations to operate their business, therefore, if a group of professionals wanted to work together, they had no choice but to form a general partnership. As discussed in Chapter 1, a disadvantage of the general partnership is the unlimited personal liability of the partners for the debts of the business.

The law was subsequently changed to permit professionals to incorporate, however, many firms feared that converting from one business form to another would be too complex to undertake, and could potentially trigger a costly taxable event under federal tax law. The limited liability partnership (LLP) was developed in response to lobbying by these professionals for a business form similar to the limited liability company (LLC).

The law now provides a simple and inexpensive way for a general partnership to convert to an LLP, avoiding many of the problems the general partnership faced when it was finally allowed to convert the business to a corporation. The general partnership simply has to register with the state as an LLP. The old general partnership is not dissolved, but instead continues to exist subject to the laws governing an LLP. Thus, conversion does not trigger a taxable event because a new entity is not created during conversion.

FEATURES OF THE LIMITED LIABILITY PARTNERSHIP

The limited liability partnership (LLP) is similar to a limited liability company (LLC) in that it enjoys certain advantageous features of both the partnership and the corporation. For example, LLP owners have limited liability for company debts, however, in many states, LLP owners only have a "reduced" form of limited liability that is not as broad as that enjoyed by shareholders of a corporation or members of an LLC. In addition, the LLP is not taxed like a corporation—there is no double taxation. Further, unlike a limited partnership, all partners can take an active role in managing the business.

In some states, such as New York and California, the LLP form of business is reserved for professionals that require a license to conduct business, such as doctors, lawyers, and accountants, who were previously prohibited from forming an LLC. Therefore, the reader is advised to check the law of his or her jurisdiction to find out whether they are eligible to form an LLP.

In the majority of states, where non-professionals are permitted to form an LLP, it is important to find out whether the state is one that provides for a reduced form of limited liability—generally referred to as a "limited shield" state—or whether the quality of the limited liability is the same for both the LLC and LLP. The following states are "limited shield" states:

Alaska
Arkansas
District of Columbia
Hawaii
Illinois
Kansas
Kentucky
Louisiana
Maine
Michigan
Nevada
New Hampshire
New Jersey
North Carolina
Ohio
Pennsylvania
South Carolina
Tennessee
Texas
Utah
West Virginia

Since your business does not have to be registered in the same state where you do business, it is inadvisable to register your LLP in one of these "limited shield" states.

NAMING YOUR LLP

You should take the same precautions in naming your LLP as are discussed in Chapter 4: Naming Your LLP. In addition, most states require the name to include a designation that shows the legal status of the business, such as "limited liability partnership" or the abbreviation "LLC," e.g., Jones, Smith and Jackson, LLP or Jones, Smith and Jackson, a Limited Liability Partnership.

TAXATION

The LLP does not pay any taxes, however, it does have to file a tax return. Any income or loss reflected on the LLP tax return is "passed through" to the LLP partners in proportion to their ownership interest in the LLP. This income must be accounted for on the individual tax returns of the LLP partners.

An LLP can elect to be taxed as a corporation, however this defeats one of the main reasons for forming an LLP. When taxed as a corporation, the income of the LLP is subject to the corporate "double-tax,"—i.e., the income is taxed once directly to the LLP and then taxed again to the partners as part of their individual income when they receive distributions from the profits of the LLP.

If no election is designated, the IRS will treat income from the LLP as "pass-through" income to the individual partners.

FORMING AN LLP

Once you have decided to form an LLP, you must register your LLP, pay any required registration fees, and fulfill various requirements of the state in which you register. For example, some states require proof that the partnership has obtained adequate liability insurance or has adequate assets to satisfy potential claims.

A sample LLP Certificate of Registration is set forth at Appendix 3.

In the majority of states, where non-professionals are permitted to form an LLP, a partnership that renders professional services may form an LLP and also register as a professional limited liability partnership (PLLP). A PLLP is the same as an LLP but the PLLP designation denotes a partnership consisting solely of professionals. Each state specifies which professions are eligible to register as a PLLP, but generally they include lawyers, doctors, dentists, accountants, architects and engineers.

Many states have a publication requirement. For example, in New York, a newly formed LLP is required, within 120 days of registration, to publish a copy of the certificate of registration, or a notice related to the registration, in two newspapers that have been designated by the county clerk of the county where the LLP's principal office is located. After publication, the newspaper provides the LLP owners with an affidavit of publication that must be filed with the state.

A sample LLP Certificate of Publication is set forth at Appendix 4.

Following registration, it is advisable for the partners to hold an organizational meeting at which time the LLP Operating Agreement can be adopted and partnership certificates can be issued. Nevertheless, there is generally no requirement that an LLP adopt a written agreement. An agreement is preferable in order to document important managerial and financial agreements among the partners. In addition, a partnership agreement allows the partners some flexibility to operate the LLP in ways that would not be permitted by law without an agreement.

The LLP agreement may address matters such as management of the LLP, distribution of profits and losses, allocation of taxable income and loss, transfer of partners' ownership interests in the LLP, and termination of the LLP. If an LLP does not have a written agreement, or the agreement does not cover a particular matter, then the LLP must be operated strictly in accordance with the LLP law of the state in which the LLP is registered.

DISSOLVING THE LLP

An LLP is generally dissolved by filing the appropriate form with the state in which the LLP is registered. The form may be called a Certificate of Dissolution, a Notice of Change, or a Certificate of Withdrawal, depending on the state.

A sample Certificate of Withdrawal of an LLP is set forth at Appendix 5.

CHAPTER 4:
NAMING YOUR LIMITED
LIABILITY COMPANY

IN GENERAL

Naming your business may seem simple, but it is actually one of the most important tasks you need to undertake when forming your LLC. Generally, you should choose a business name that is easy to remember, simple to pronounce, and one that will help identify your LLC's products and/or services. However, you can't just choose any name you like. When it comes to naming your LLC, you have to do some research. For example, you cannot use a name that can be confused with a similar business, or you risk being sued for trademark infringement, as further discussed below. In addition, there are state and local regulations regarding business names.

LEGAL REQUIREMENTS

Each business structure has its own rules when it comes to selecting a name. For example, a sole proprietor must generally use his or her own name unless the owner formally files another name as a "d/b/a—doing business as"—trade name, e.g., Mary Jones d/b/a Jones Real Estate.

Similarly, when you form your LLC, you must select a name that complies with your state's regulations for LLC business names. In most states, the following rules apply:

Prohibited or Restricted Words

You cannot use any words that are prohibited or restricted by the state. For example, the word "insurance" is generally prohibited unless the name makes it clear that the business is not an insurance company. In addition, the name is usually required to be written in English letters or Arabic or Roman numerals.

LLC Designation

Just as a corporation must contain the word "corporation," "inc.," "limited," or comparable words or abbreviations, the name of a limited liability company must end with a word or abbreviation that designates the business as a limited liability company, e.g., "limited liability company" or "limited liability co.," or the abbreviation "L.L.C." or "LLC". For example, you cannot use Jones Real Estate without an appropriate LLC designator—e.g., Jones Real Estate, LLC, or Jones Real Estate, a Limited Liability Company.

Distinguishable Name

The proposed name must be distinguishable from the name of any other corporation, cooperative, limited liability company, limited partnership, or limited liability partnership registered with the state. For example, the Wisconsin Secretary of State gives the following examples of distinguishable (acceptable) and indistinguishable (unacceptable) name variations:

Distinguishable and Acceptable

Transfer Technology Corp. is distinguishable from Technology Transfer Inc.

Small Business Services, Inc. is distinguishable from Small Business Systems, Inc.

Roberts Construction, LLC is distinguishable from Roberts Construction Assoc., LLC.

Smith Carriers, Inc. is distinguishable from New Smith Carriers, Inc.

Indistinguishable and Unacceptable

A.A.A. Cleaners Company is indistinguishable from AAA Cleaners Inc.

Amer Inc. is indistinguishable from Amer Co., Inc.

ABC, Limited Liability Company is indistinguishable from ABC, Corporation.

Business Machines Limited is indistinguishable from Business Machines LLC.

Same or Similar Names

The proposed name cannot be the same, or deceptively similar, to another company name. For example, the Wisconsin Secretary of State gives the following examples of acceptable and unacceptable name variations:

Not Deceptively Similar and Acceptable

Halifax Wholesale Limited Partnership is not deceptively similar to Halifax Outlet Limited Partnership.

Ford Dealers Association, Limited Partnership is not deceptively similar to Wisconsin Dealers Association, Ltd.

Walworth Parks Committee Limited Partnership is not deceptively similar to Park Users of Walworth, LLC.

Deceptively Similar and Unacceptable

St. Croix County Development Limited Partnership is deceptively similar to St. Croix Development Limited Partnership.

Selkirk, Huxtable and Simmons Limited Partnership is deceptively similar to Selkirk, Huxtable, Simmons & Assoc. Limited Partnership.

Contractor's Funding Limited Partnership is deceptively similar to Contracting Fund Limited Partnership.

RESEARCHING YOUR PROPOSED NAME

As discussed below, before you finalize an official business name for your LLC, you must first find out whether the name, or a similar name, is already in use. If the name is not in use, it is advisable to file a fictitious or assumed business name statement with your county clerk's office, and register the business name for protection at both the state and federal level.

Local Use

You should check with your county clerk's office to see whether your proposed business name is on the list of fictitious or assumed business names in your county. In some states, the list of fictitious names is contained in a statewide database. The list contains the names of unregistered trademarks of small companies that you won't find in any other databases. If you find that your chosen name is listed on a local fictitious or assumed name list, it is advisable to choose an alternate name.

Statewide Use

The official business name for an LLC is registered with the state Secretary of State where the LLC is doing business. In general, the business name is automatically registered with the state when the LLC articles of organization are filed. You can check the availability of your proposed name by contacting the Secretary of State. An LLC cannot use a business name that is the same as that of an existing LLC in the state where it is registered.

When you register your LLC name with the Secretary of State's office, you should also have an alternative name in case your first choice is not available. Although registration may create a public record of your use of a business name, registering the name does not establish or reserve exclusive rights to use of the name.

A directory of state Secretaries of State is set forth at Appendix 6.

RESERVING YOUR LLC NAME

If your proposed LLC name is available, but you are not ready to file your Articles of Organization, you may be able to reserve the LLC name. Most states require that you file an application for name reservation, along with a filing fee. The name will be reserved for a period of time, e.g., 60 days, until you are ready to file your Articles of Organization. During this time, no other person can use the reserved name. When you file your Articles of Organization, you should attach your name reservation filing receipt.

A sample Application for Reservation of LLC Name is set forth at Appendix 7.

FEDERAL TRADEMARK PROTECTION

For LLCs that want to do business outside of the local marketplace, a name may be registered as a trademark through the U.S. Patent and Trademark Office (USPTO). The USPTO maintains a free online search feature that allows the user to search all of the state and federal registers to find out if the name is already being used. If your proposed name is not already registered with the USPTO, you can apply for trademark protection that will prevent another business from using your chosen business name, and any name that is likely to be confused with it. This is advantageous if you plan on marketing your product or service to a widespread population.

Although federal registration is not required to establish rights in a name or to begin using the name, registration can secure benefits beyond the rights acquired by merely using the name. For example, the owner of a federal registration is presumed to be the owner of the name for the goods and services specified in the registration, and to be entitled to use the name nationwide. Further, federal registration places the public on notice of the registrant's claim of ownership of the name. In fact, after five years of registration, a trademark attains an "incontestible status" which eliminates most arguments that the registrant does not have the exclusive right to utilize the name.

In addition, it is only through federal registration that the owner of a name has the right to use the "Registered" ("®") symbol. Use of this symbol is advantageous in that it will likely deter potential trademark infringers.

Further, federal registration can be used as a basis for obtaining registration in foreign countries, and may be filed with U.S. Customs Service to prevent importation of infringing foreign goods.

As further discussed below, federal registration also invokes federal court jurisdiction and allows the registrant to recover profits, damages and costs for infringement, including the possibility of receiving treble damages under certain circumstances; and the ability to recover legal fees in infringement actions.

Trademark Protection Requirements

In order to be eligible for trademark protection, the name must be "distinctive," not common or ordinary. For example, "White Castle" is distinctive, but "John's Hamburgers" would be considered ordinary. Small businesses are advised to use names that the customer can remember easily, and that are in some way associated with the products or services offered by the company. The name should be easy to spell and pronounce, and must not infringe on an existing name.

For example, you should not use part of a well-known name even if your business does not offer the same products or services, e.g., "IBM Candies, Inc." If the company owning the name prevails in an infringement lawsuit, at the very least, you will be stuck with the cost of reprinting all of your signage and advertising materials. At worst, you will incur legal fees defending the lawsuit, and face a possible money judgment that could bankrupt your company before it has a chance to get started.

If the name you choose is not so famous or recognizable, but turns out to be the same or similar to an existing name, you may still be able to use it if the company who owns the name is using it in a totally different context, e.g., your business is a hair salon called "Lemon Tree," and someone else uses the same name for a business that imports citrus fruit.

If you decide to use your surname in your business name, it would not be given protection as a trademark unless it achieved secondary meaning through prolonged use or extensive advertising. Once the surname achieves secondary meaning, the trademark may gain protection and third parties will be prohibited from using the name on confusingly similar goods, even if they have the same surname. Thus, Joe "Hilton" cannot name his hotel, "Hilton Hotel."

The Trademark Search

An applicant for trademark registration is advised to conduct a thorough search to determine whether or not the trademark they intend to register has been previously registered or is subject to common law trademark rights. If a search is not performed, a trademark owner with prior rights may force the new mark to be discontinued. By the time this occurs, the applicant may have spent a lot of money in advertising and marketing.

The scope of a trademark search should be broad and include investigation into federal trademark registrations, state trademark registrations, and common law trademark rights. Because U.S. trademark rights are based on "use" not "registration," the search of federal and state registries should include pending and abandoned applications, and expired registrations. For example, even though a registration may be expired, the mark may nevertheless be protected because it may still be in use.

Unregistered Names

A search of common law unregistered trademarks is important for the same reason. There are many companies doing business that do not bother to register their business names at all, therefore, you won't find them in any of the local, state or federal databases. Common law rights arise from actual use of a mark. Thus, the first party to use a mark in commerce will generally have the ultimate right to register that mark. Nevertheless, common law trademark rights are limited to the geographic area in which the mark is used.

Although it is almost impossible to find out whether your proposed name is the same or similar to an unregistered business name, you can take some precaution by checking phone directories, yellow pages, industrial directories, state trademark registers, among other databases, in an effort to determine if a particular mark is used by others who have not filed for a federal trademark registration. You should also search the Internet to see whether your proposed name is in use, by entering variations of your proposed name in a search engine or checking an Internet domain name registrar, as further discussed below.

There are also trademark search firms and trademark attorneys that perform trademark searches for a fee. Although it is possible and permissible to perform the trademark search on your own, the results will generally not be as thorough as a search conducted by a professional service.

Trademark Infringement

Trademark infringement generally occurs when a third party's use of a trademark causes confusion about the source of the goods or services involved. Multiple parties may use the same name only when the goods or services of the parties are not so similar as to cause confusion among consumers.

The elements for a successful trademark infringement claim are well-established. The plaintiff must prove that the defendant's use of a trademark has created a likelihood-of-confusion about the origin of the defendant's goods or services. The plaintiff must demonstrate that it has a right in the trademark and that the defendant is using a confusingly similar mark in such a way that it creates a likelihood of confusion, mistake and/or deception with the consumers.

There are eight factors that generally determine likelihood of confusion:

1. The similarity in the overall impression created by the two trademarks;

2. The similarities of the goods and services involved;

3. The strength of the plaintiff's trademark;

4. Evidence of actual confusion by consumers;

5. The intent of the defendant in adopting its trademark;

6. The physical proximity of the goods in the retail marketplace;

7. The degree of care likely to be exercised by the consumer in distinguishing the goods and/or services; and

8. The likelihood of expansion of the product lines.

Although the similarity of the marks is a significant part in establishing likelihood of confusion, it is still possible for an identical mark to be used in the same geographic area without any trademark infringement occurring provided the goods or services of the parties are sufficiently dissimilar.

Infringement Under the Common Law

Unlike federally registered marks which have nationwide protection, marks which are protected under common law rights are limited to the geographic area in which the mark is used—i.e., there can be no geographic overlap in the use of the marks.

For example, if a house cleaning service called "Happy Household Helpers" is formed solely in New York, the common-law trademark rights in that name exist only in New York. A house cleaning service located in California who had no knowledge of the New York service is free to use the same name, and there is no trademark infringement. However, if the service wanted to expand nationwide, a search may reveal the existence of the New York company. The California service would thus be prevented from using the mark in New York or risk an infringement action by the New York company.

Hershey v. Hershey

The following case illustrates the importance of choosing a name for your LLC that cannot be confused with an existing business name, particularly if the products and/or services are similar. Hershey Foods Corp. v. Hershey Creamery Co., 945 F.2d 1272 (3d Cir. 1991), involves two very well-known brands. Hershey Creamery Co. is an ice cream company founded by Jacob Hershey and his brothers. To this day, many consumers mistakenly assume that Hershey Ice Cream is connected to the more famous chocolate candy company, Hershey Foods Corp., which was founded by Milton S. Hershey. In fact, both companies were started in 1894 in Pennsylvania. Although the founders were related, the companies are not, and consumer confusion and trademark litigation have been an issue between the two companies ever since they began.

Hershey Foods was the first to register the name "Hershey's" with the United States Patent and Trademark Office in 1906. Under the registered trademark, the Company manufactured and sold candy, chocolate, cocoa, chocolate milk, chocolate syrup, and refrigerated puddings. In 1910, the Hershey brothers, who later founded Hershey Creamery, began manufacturing and selling ice cream products, using the same "Hershey's" trademark.

In 1921, Hershey Foods filed the first lawsuit between these parties and five years later, the district court issued a decree enjoining the Hershey brothers from using the trademark "Hershey's" in connection with the manufacture, advertisement, distribution, or sale of, among other things, chocolate, cocoa, chocolate confections, and chocolate or cocoa products.

In 1958, Hershey Creamery successfully registered the "Hershey's" trademark for the manufacture and sale of ice cream and butter. In 1966, Hershey Creamery filed a trademark infringement lawsuit when it learned that Hershey Foods was planning to enter the ice cream business by granting another company the right to use the "Hershey's" trademark on ice cream bars coated with chocolate. In response, Hershey Foods filed a counterclaim challenging the validity of Hershey Creamery's trademark registration for ice cream and butter.

In 1967, a settlement was reached whereby Hershey Creamery agreed to drop its claims against Hershey Foods and allow Hershey Foods to license its "Hershey's" trademark for use in connection with ice cream bars. In return, Hershey Foods agreed not to attack the validity of Hershey Creamery's trademark "Hershey's" for ice cream.

Shortly thereafter, Hershey Creamery obtained an additional trademark registration of "Hershey's" for various ice cream products, including "ice cream, ice milk, sherbet, water ice, and frozen confections in which ice cream, ice milk, sherbet or water ice is a component." In 1989, Hershey Creamery began to sell and advertise frozen yogurt in containers bearing the mark "Hershey's" and filed another application in the United States Patent and Trademark Office to register the trademark for that product.

When Hershey Foods became aware of the application to register "Hershey's" as a trademark for frozen yogurt, it threatened an infringement action and requested that Hershey Creamery discontinue use of the name "Hershey's" on the frozen yogurt. Although Hershey Creamery withdrew its pending application for registration of the mark for frozen yogurt, it refused to discontinue use of the name "Hershey's" in connection with the advertisement and sale of frozen yogurt.

Hershey Foods retained a consumer research expert to assess the level of potential confusion caused by Hershey Creamery's use of "Hershey's" for frozen yogurt and ice cream. This expert found that 76.7% of 223 purchasers of frozen yogurt and 88.6% of 228 purchasers of ice cream in the thirteen states where Hershey Creamery trades believed that the frozen yogurt and ice cream were the products of Hershey Foods. It is likely that infringement lawsuits will continue between the two companies as they develop new products. In the meantime, the Hershey Creamery has placed the following notation on its website: "Products of Hershey Creamery Co.—Not affiliated with Hershey's Chocolate."

REGISTERING AN INTERNET DOMAIN NAME FOR YOUR LLC

The Domain Name System (DNS) can best be described as the Internet's phone book consisting of millions of domain names. A domain name is a unique text name linked to a numerical "address" of another computer that stores web pages on the Internet (a "web server"). Basically, when an Internet user types a domain name into their computer, a software program on the user's computer (a "web browser") connects to the web server. The web server then transmits the web pages back to the user's computer where the pages are displayed. For example, you can access my website by typing the domain name "www.JasperLawOffice.com/."

If you plan to do business on the Worldwide Web, you should find out whether the trade name you have chosen is available as an Internet domain name before you settle on the name. For example, if Mary Jones wants to advertise the services of her company, Jones Real Estate, on the Internet, she must choose a unique domain name that links to the company website. An obvious choice for the domain name would be "www.JonesRealEstate.com/." If that name is taken, Mary Jones will have to choose an alternate domain name. The domain name you choose must be unique, and should contain all or part of your proposed business name so that your website will be easier to locate.

If you want to register a domain name for your LLC, you must first conduct a domain name search to see whether the name is "available." You can search for available domain names by visiting a company known as a domain name registrar, such as "godaddy.com." In some cases, if the name is "taken," you can purchase the domain name from the person or entity holding it.

If the name is available—i.e., no other person or company has registered the domain name—or you are able to purchase the domain name, you may register the domain name as your own. For a small fee, a domain registrar will host the domain name and prevent individuals from registering the same name.

Once you have a registered domain name for your LLC, you can "publish" your LLC's website on the worldwide web. There are services that will build a website for you, or you can create a website on your own using certain software. Once you are satisfied with how your website looks and operates, you would submit it to a web hosting service—i.e., a company that makes your website available to Internet users for a hosting fee. When the Internet user enters your domain name, the user's computer accesses your company's website and displays your web pages on the user's computer screen.

Trademark Infringement on the Internet

Claims of trademark infringement are increasing in large part due to the use of the Internet and World Wide Web. The most significant source of Internet infringement allegations concerns domain names, as described above. When a domain name dispute arises, the party seeking to obtain the existing domain name generally relies on trademark rights. In most of these cases, the existing domain name is identical to a company's well-established trademark. Nevertheless, this does not necessarily prove trademark infringement because the existing website may have absolutely nothing to do with the goods and services offered by the company trying to obtain the domain name.

CHAPTER 5:
THE LLC ARTICLES OF ORGANIZATION

WHAT ARE ARTICLES OF ORGANIZATION?

The Articles of Organization establish the existence of your LLC in your state, and set forth certain basic information about your company. The Articles of Organization describe the organizational and operational details of your LLC. Your LLC is legally created once the Articles of Organization are filed and approved by your state. In some states, the Articles of Organization document is called a "Certificate of Organization" or a "Certificate of Formation."

The Articles of Organization are not particularly complicated, and will likely be accepted for filing as long as they contain the minimum amount of information required by your state. Although state laws may vary, most states require the LLC Articles of Organization to include the following basic information:

1. The name of the LLC;

2. The address of the LLC's principal place of business;

3. The nature of the business conducted by the LLC. This may be stated in broad language, e.g., "to engage in any lawful activity under the laws of the state of [insert state name]." The language is purposely broad so that the LLC is not limited to a strictly-defined business venture.

4. The name and address of the registered agent for the LLC.

5. The names of the members and managers of the LLC.

In addition, the Articles of Organization usually identify the organizer of the LLC. The organizer is the person typically responsible for signing the Articles of Organization and filing them with the state. A limited liability company may have more than one organizer. The organizers may or may not be the same as the members of the LLC. All of the LLC members may prepare and sign the Articles or Organization, or they can appoint an individual to do so on behalf of the LLC.

Most states offer a pre-printed Articles of Organization form, which contains fill-in spaces for all of the required information. You have the option of using the state form or completing your own Articles of Organization to meet your specific needs.

Sample Articles of Organization forms for a domestic limited liability company (LLC) and professional limited liability company (PLLC) are set forth at Appendices 8 and 9, respectively.

APPOINTMENT OF A REGISTERED AGENT

The Articles of Organization generally require the appointment of the LLC's registered agent for the service of process. The registered agent is the person authorized to accept delivery of certain legal documents, such as a summons and complaint, in case the LLC is sued. The registered agent is usually one of the LLC members. Some states also allow an LLC to designate the Secretary of State as the LLC's registered agent.

MANAGEMENT CLAUSE

As set forth above, the Articles of Organization must list the members and managers of the LLC. The members may directly manage the LLC or they may vest management in one or more managers. Managers need not be LLC members. Under most state laws, unless the Articles of Organization vest management of the LLC in one or more managers, management of the LLC is conducted by the LLC members, subject to any provisions set forth in the LLC Operating Agreement, if there is one. If there is no Operating Agreement, state law controls. For this reason, when forming an LLC, it is advisable to draft an Operating Agreement for the LLC in addition to the Articles of Organization.

Following is a typical state law concerning management of an LLC:

Wisconsin Statutes—Subchapter IV. Rights and Duties of Members and Managers

Section 183.0401 Management.

Unless the articles of organization vest management of a limited liability company in one or more managers, management of the limited liability company shall be vested in the members, subject to any provision in an operating agreement or this chapter restricting or enlarging the management rights and duties of any member or group of members.

Section 183.0401(2)

If the articles of organization vest management of a limited liability company in one or more managers, management of the business or affairs of the limited liability company shall be vested in the manager or managers, subject to any provisions in an operating agreement or this chapter restricting or enlarging the management rights and duties of any manager or group of managers. Unless otherwise provided in an operating agreement, the manager or managers:

(a) Shall be designated, appointed, elected, removed or replaced by a vote of the members that meets the requirements under Section 183.0404(1)(a).

(b) Need not be members of the limited liability company or individuals.

(c) Shall hold office until a successor is elected and qualified, or until prior death, resignation or removal.

FILING THE ARTICLES OF ORGANIZATION

Once you have written your LLC's Articles of Organization, you must file them with the state agency responsible for handling business registrations. In most states, this is the office of the Secretary of State. The required filing fee must accompany the Articles of Organization. The amount of the fee varies according to the state in which your LLC is located.

A table of state LLC filing fees is set forth at Appendix 10.

If your paperwork is in order, you will be issued an official filing receipt. The filing receipt will contain certain information, such as the date of filing, the name of the LLC, an extract of information provided in the Articles of Organization, and an accounting of the fees paid. You should verify that this information is correct. The filing receipt is your proof of filing, therefore, you should keep it in a safe place. Some state agencies will not issue duplicate filing receipts if the original is lost or destroyed.

PUBLICATION REQUIREMENT

In some states, including Arizona, Nebraska, New York and Pennsylvania, an LLC must publish a notice regarding the formation of the LLC before filing the Articles of Organization, or within a certain number of days after filing. New York State's publication requirement is the strictest among the states, as follows:

New York Publication Requirement

Pursuant to Section 206 of the New York Limited Liability Company Law, every LLC, LLP, LP or PLLC must publish a detailed notice in one daily newspaper and one weekly newspaper, to be determined by the clerk of the county in which the LLC or LLP intends to operate. The notice must run once per week for four weeks, and must contain the following information:

1. The name of the LLC.

2. The date the Articles of Organization were filed.

3. The county where the LLC's principal office is located.

4. A statement that the Secretary of State has been designated as an agent of process for the LLC.

5. The address where any process served on the Secretary of State may be forwarded to the LLC.

6. The name and address of the LLC's registered agent for service of process.

7. Date of dissolution, if applicable.

8. Character and purpose of the LLC.

9. The names of the LLC's ten largest owners who are actively engaged in the business and affairs of the LLC.

The publication requirement must be completed within 120 days of filing. A Certificate of Publication, along with the affidavits of publication from each of the two newspapers, and the required filing fee, must be filed with the Secretary of State. The Affidavits of Publication must comply with the following requirements:

1. The Affidavit of Publication must not include the actual clipping of the newspaper publication. The statute only requires that the text of the publication be in or annexed to the Affidavit of Publication. A photocopy of the newspaper clipping may be attached to the Affidavit of Publication if it is of sufficient size and otherwise suitable for microfilming or other imaging technology.

2. The newspaper should print the text of the publication on white paper to be attached to the Affidavit of Publication or include the text of the publication in the Affidavit of Publication.

3. Small font size is not permitted. A font size of 10 or larger should be used.

4. The Affidavit of Publication and attached copy of the publication, if applicable, must be on 8 ½ x 11 paper.

5. The Affidavit of Publication may include only one copy of the text of the publication, not a copy of each week's publication.

If the LLC fails to publish the required notice and file proof of publication to the Secretary of State within the 120-day period after formation, the LLC will automatically be suspended.

Sample Certificates of Publication for a domestic limited liability company (LLC) and a professional limited liability company (PLLC) are set forth at Appendices 11 and 12, respectively.

CHAPTER 6:
THE LLC OPERATING AGREEMENT

IN GENERAL

An LLC operating agreement is an important internal document setting forth the rights and responsibilities of the LLC members to each other and to the LLC. The operating agreement specifies each member's percentage of interest in the business, and their individual share of the profits or losses. The operating agreement also details how the LLC will be managed, what will happen if one or more LLC members decides to leave the LLC, and the procedures for adding additional members to the LLC.

Even if you are the sole member of the LLC, it is advisable to create an operating agreement to separate you, as an individual, from your business. This is particularly important to protect your limited liability status. Without the formality of an operating agreement, your business may appear more like a sole proprietorship than an LLC. In addition, an operating agreement lends credibility to your business, particularly when you apply for financing.

In most states, an LLC is not required to adopt or file an operating agreement. However, if you do not create an operating agreement for your company, the LLC law of the state in which your LLC is registered will govern. For example, many states will require the LLC to apportion profits and losses equally if there is no operating agreement that specifies a different split among the members. This is so even if you can show that you invested the most money in the LLC. The only way to make sure your LLC is run the way you want is to prepare an operating agreement to govern your business.

PREPARING THE LLC OPERATING AGREEMENT

In general, most LLC operating agreements include the following provisions:

1. How the LLC will be managed;

2. Each member's rights and responsibilities;

3. Each member's percentage of ownership in the LLC;

4. The apportionment of profits and losses;

5. Rules for LLC meetings;

6. The voting rights of each member;

7. The procedure to follow if a member wants to leave the LLC and sell his or her interest;

8. The procedure to follow if a member passes away or becomes disabled and unable to participate in the LLC;

9. Buyout provisions for a leaving member; and

10. The procedure for dissolving the LLC.

MANAGEMENT OF THE LLC

The operating agreement should describe how the business will be managed, including the rights and responsibilities of each of the members to each other, and to the LLC. In most LLCs, the members participate equally in managing the company, however, this is not a requirement of the LLC. The operating agreement can assign management responsibilities to one or more of the members, while other members assume a more inactive role in the day-to-day operations of the company.

PERCENTAGE OF OWNERSHIP

If more than one person decides to form an LLC, each member generally contributes something to the business, either in the form of cash, property or services. In return, each member is given a percentage of ownership interest in the LLC, generally in proportion to the amount he or she contributed. However, the members are free to agree to apportion the ownership interests in any way they choose.

For example, it may be that Member A's financial contribution is much more valuable than Member B's contribution of property, or that Member C's expertise in running the business is more crucial than Member A's financial contribution.

It is important to specify the appropriate ownership shares among the members. Without such a provision, if ownership becomes an issue, the law of the state will govern, and each member will likely be credited with an equal share in the business regardless of the value of his or her individual contribution.

DISTRIBUTION OF PROFITS AND LOSSES

In addition to specifying the ownership interests in the LLC, the operating agreement should also set forth each member's share of the profits and losses of the LLC. In general, this percentage usually corresponds with the percentage of ownership. For example, if Member A is given 45% ownership in the business, and Member B is given 55% ownership, then Member A will be allocated 45% of the profits and losses, and Member B will be allocated to 55% of the profits and losses.

If you want to divide profit and losses in a way that does not correspond to the members' ownership interests in the LLC, you must follow the special allocation rules set forth by the Internal Revenue Service (IRS). The IRS special allocation rules are designed to prevent LLC members from shifting income to avoid taxes, e.g., if the LLC allocates all or most of the LLC's losses to a member who is in the highest income tax bracket.

If the IRS determines that the special allocation was made to avoid taxes, it will reject the special allocation and tax all of the members in proportion to their ownership interests in the LLC regardless of the profit and loss distribution provision of the LLC operating agreement.

In addition to the profit and loss distribution, the LLC operating agreement should also set forth whether LLC profits will be distributed to the members or whether they will be reinvested in the business. Even if the profits are reinvested and not distributed, each member is still required to pay income taxes on the amount of profits allocated. Therefore, the operating agreement must also specify whether the members will receive enough income from the LLC to cover the amount of income tax they will be required to pay based on their profit allocation.

MEETINGS

The operating agreement should set forth the conduct of the LLC meetings, which may be as formal or as informal as the members desire. For example, the operating agreement can require the LLC to hold regular meetings and also require that all members be given formal notice of any meeting. The operating agreement can require minutes to be taken at the meetings, and the recording of key decisions concerning LLC management.

VOTING RIGHTS

Obviously, a one-member LLC does not have to be concerned with voting rights, however, an LLC with two or more members may find themselves in disagreement on how to resolve an issue involving the LLC. Therefore, the operating agreement should set forth the voting rights of the LLC members.

Generally, most LLCs specify that a member's voting rights will correspond to his or her ownership interest in the LLC. Alternatively, the LLC can specify a one vote per member provision. In addition, the operating agreement should state whether the vote on an issue must be unanimous or by a majority in order to prevail.

BUYOUT PROVISIONS

The operating agreement should also set forth buyout provisions in case a member passes away, becomes disabled, or retires. For example, the operating agreement can provide that a leaving member's ownership interest cannot be sold to a non-member, or that the interest must be sold back to the LLC.

TERMINATION

The operating agreement should also set forth the terms under which the LLC may be dissolved, e.g., by a majority vote, and the amount of compensation the individual members will be entitled to upon dissolution.

A sample LLC operating agreement is set forth at Appendix 13.

CHAPTER 7:
FINANCING YOUR LIMITED
LIABILITY COMPANY

IN GENERAL

One of the most important aspects of operating a business is maintaining adequate cash flow. One of the leading causes of business failure is insufficient start-up capital. If the business takes off, more money will be needed to carry the increased operational costs, which may include additional inventory and payroll, as well as expansion funds. Basically, you should have enough money to cover the operating expenses of your company for at least one year.

Many small business owners use their own money to start their new businesses. Personal savings should be considered the primary source of funds for starting a business. If you haven't started already, start now to begin accumulating cash through personal savings. Overall, small firms rely more on owner capital and less on external debt capital than larger firms.

In addition, small firms are more dependent than large firms on short-term debt relative to long-term debt. Most small firms use external financing only occasionally. Less than half of small firms borrow once or more during a year. However, small firms experiencing rapid growth or those with high volumes of receivables require frequent external financing. Thus, unless personal funds are unlimited, you will have to look to outside financing at some point to keep the business afloat.

RAISING CAPITAL

The capital you are seeking to raise will likely be a combination of debt capital and equity capital. Debt capital is the money you raise through loans that are repaid with interest, usually through a bank. Equity capital is the money you raise by giving up some portion of ownership in your business, such as through a partnership arrangement.

There should be a balance between your debt and equity capital, since too much of either can be bad. If you incur too much debt capital, your company will look unstable, and it is unlikely you will be able to obtain any more financing should the need arise. If you raise too much equity capital, you run the risk of losing control of your business to the investors, who generally require a provision allowing them to replace you if they suspect that you are unable to adequately manage the business.

As set forth below, before you apply for any kind of financing, there are steps you should take to present your company and your personal financial affairs in the best light possible. This will increase your chances of securing financing.

Your Credit History

When you apply for bank financing, one of the first things the bank will determine is whether your personal and business credit is good. Therefore before you start the loan application process, you want to make sure your credit is good. First you must obtain a copy of your personal credit reports from each of the three major credit reporting agencies.

Contact information for the three major national credit reporting agencies is as follows:

EQUIFAX
P.O. Box 740241
Atlanta, GA 30374
Tel: (800) 685-1111
Website: www.equifax.com

EXPERIAN
701 Experian Parkway
Allen, TX 75013
Tel: (888) 397-3742
Website: www.experian.com

TRANS UNION
P.O. Box 1000
Chester, PA 19022
Tel: (800) 916-8800
Website: www.transunion.com

It is important that you obtain your credit reports well in advance of applying for a loan. Personal credit reports may contain errors or outdated information. It may take up to 3 or 4 weeks to have erroneous items corrected. You want to make sure that when the bank requests your credit report, all of the errors have been corrected and your credit history is up to date.

When you review your credit report, make sure your name, social security number and address are correct. Also review all of the entries for credit you have obtained in the past, such as credit cards, car loans, mortgages, student loans, etc.

Any negative credit entry, such as a charge-off, late payment, judgment, etc., will be listed on your credit report and will affect your ability to qualify for credit. If a specific event e.g., an illness or divorce—contributed to negative credit entries, and you can show that your credit prior to and following the event was good, you should add an explanation on your credit report and also attach the explanation to your loan application.

Your Credit Score

The credit score—also known as a risk score—is an individual's statistically derived numerical value used by a lender to predict the likelihood of certain credit behaviors, including default. The credit score summarizes your credit payment history, number of open accounts, overall credit balances and public records such as judgments and liens. In addition, factors such as late payments and the number of inquiries in your credit file can lower your credit score and lead to a denial of credit.

Credit scores—which are made up of three digits— range from a low of 365 to a high of 850. Generally, a score above 680 will produce a positive response while a score below this will cause a lender to be cautious. It is advisable to find out what your credit score is before applying for a business loan. You can obtain your credit score through any one of the three major credit-reporting agencies listed above.

Prepare a Comprehensive Business Plan

The bank will want some assurance that the business will be able to repay the loan. You should demonstrate your experience and track record in the particular business by preparing a comprehensive business plan to accompany your loan package. The business plan should precisely describe your business, including your product or service, key employees of the company, the market, the costs, potential profit, etc. The new business owner will have to demonstrate to the lender or investor the potential of the new business in order to obtain funding. A well-developed business plan is essential in this regard and is a crucial part of any loan package.

The purpose of your business plan is to precisely define your business, its goals, and its potential. It should show your company in the best possible light, without being misleading, and without divulging too much information should a competitor get his or her hands on it. A properly drawn business plan should include as its basic components your company's balance sheets, income statements, and cash flow analyses.

Before you begin formulating your business plan, there are certain steps you should follow:

1. Research your proposed business in detail, including the market, the competition, the sales and profit potential and the amount of start-up money you will need for your particular type of business;

2. Research the location where you will establish your business to make sure it is appropriate for the type of business you are proposing—location can make or break a new business;

3. Gather complete business records, including all financial data that relates to your business.

4. Define your goals and objectives.

A well-organized business plan should include the following components:

Introduction

The introduction should give a detailed description of the business and its goals and discuss the ownership of the business and the legal structure, e.g., the company is being formed as a limited liability company (LLC), professional limited liability company (PLLC), or limited liability partnership (LLP), etc. You should also list the skills and experience you bring to the business and the advantages your business has over its competition.

Marketing Section

The section on marketing should discuss the product and/or service offered; identify the customer demand for the product and/or service; and identify the market, its size and locations. You should also explain how your product and/or service will be advertised and marketed and explain the pricing strategy.

Financial Management Section

The section on financial management should explain your source and the amount of initial equity capital. It should set forth a monthly operating budget and an expected return on investment and monthly cash flow for the first year. You should provide projected income statements and balance sheets for a two-year period and discuss your break-even point. You should also explain your personal balance sheet and method of compensation. Discuss who will maintain your accounting records and how they will be kept and address alternative approaches to any problem that may develop.

Operations Section

The operations section should explain how the business will be managed on a day-to-day basis and discuss hiring and personnel procedures. Insurance, lease or rental agreements, and issues pertinent to your business should be discussed. Explain the equipment necessary to produce the products or services offered by the business, and account for production and delivery of products and services.

Concluding Statement

The concluding statement should summarize your business goals and objectives and express your commitment to the success of your business.

A sample business plan format is set forth at Appendix 14.

In addition to your comprehensive business plan, you should provide the bank with the projected cash flow for the first three years of your business and a list of collateral available to secure the loan.

Financial institutions look to collateral for a second source of repayment. Collateral are those personal and business assets that can be sold to pay back the loan. Most loan programs require at least some collateral to secure a loan. If a potential borrower has no collateral to secure a loan, he or she will need a co-signer that has collateral to pledge. Otherwise it may be difficult to obtain a loan.

The value of collateral is not based on the market value. It is discounted to take into account the value that would be lost if the assets had to be liquidated.

According to the Small Business Administration (SBA), following are the key questions a lender will ask when considering a business loan application:

1. Can the business repay the loan—e.g., is cash flow greater than debt service?

2. Can you repay the loan if the business fails—e.g., is your collateral sufficient to repay the loan?

3. Does the business collect its bills?

4. Does the business control its inventory?

5. Does the business pay its bills?

6. Are the officers committed to the business?

7. Does the business have a profitable operating history?

8. Does the business match its sources and uses of funds?

9. Are sales growing?

10. Does the business control expenses?

11. Are profits increasing as a percentage of sales?

12. Is there any discretionary cash flow?

13. What is the future of the industry?

14. Who is your competition and what are their strengths and weaknesses?

It is important to be prepared to answer these questions in order to maximize your chances for loan approval.

Demonstrate Your Personal Financial Stability

In addition to a good credit report, as discussed above, you should also illustrate your personal financial stability by providing a detailed financial statement of your own resources and expenses. If you can show that you own your own home and have had a steady source of income for a number of years, this is helpful in gaining loan approval.

A sample SBA personal financial statement is set forth at Appendix 15.

SOURCES OF DEBT CAPITAL

Access to credit is vital for small business survival. Important providers of credit to small firms include commercial banks and lending institutions, the Small Business Administration, and finance companies.

Business Loan

The primary source of debt capital you should try to obtain for your company is a business loan from a bank or other financial institution. Terms of loans may vary from lender to lender, but there are two basic types of loans: (1) a short term loan; and (2) a long term loan.

Generally, a short term loan has a maturity of up to one year. These include working capital loans, accounts receivable loans, and lines of credit. Long term loans have maturities greater than one year but usually less than seven years, although real estate and equipment loans may have maturities of up to 25 years. Long term loans are used for major business expenses such as purchasing real estate and facilities, construction, durable equipment, furniture and fixtures, vehicles, etc.

Repayment of a business loan is generally made in installments at various intervals e.g., monthly, quarterly, etc., depending on the duration of the loan.

Banks may also offer what are known as accounts receivable loans, whereby the bank lends on a percentage, e.g. 80%, of the company's outstanding invoices on a short-term basis. The invoice payments are forwarded to the bank, which deducts the loan amount plus interest and forwards the balance to the company. In some cases, the bank will act as a "factor," in which case you actually sell your accounts receivable to the bank, which assumes collection if the customers default in payment.

Applying for a Business Loan

Because banks operate on a relatively low profit margin, they are not in the practice of taking risks. Therefore, a bank is much more likely to lend money to a successful ongoing business that is seeking funds to expand operations than to a small start-up business that needs funds to get the business up and running.

To limit the bank exposure to losses if the business fails, approval of a new business bank loan—short-term or long-term—generally requires a personal guaranty of payment from the LLC owner. Thus, if the LLC defaults in its repayment of credit, the lender can go after the personal assets of the individual guarantor.

Business Line of Credit

A line of credit extended to a company by a bank or other financial institution operates in much the same way as a personal credit card. The lender will generally conduct a credit check before establishing a maximum credit line, which the company can draw upon as needed.

Trade Credit

Delaying payment to suppliers for merchandise received is a form of short-term loan. Suppliers often encourage early payment by discounting invoices that are paid within a certain specified time, e.g., 30 days. On the other hand, payments that are delayed beyond a specified time, e.g., 60 days, will usually incur interest.

Equipment Loans and Leases

When financing is needed to purchase the company's equipment, the equipment itself may serve as collateral for a loan. Alternatively, the company may enter into a leasing agreement whereby the leasing company holds title to the equipment for the duration of the lease, which generally extends for the designated life of the equipment. The company makes payments during the lease period, which in the aggregate will have exceeded the purchase price of the equipment by the end of the lease term. Depending on the lease provisions, at the end of the lease, the company may be able to take title to the equipment for a nominal sum.

The Small Business Administration Financing Assistance

The Small Business Administration (SBA) is the largest source of long term small business financing in the nation. The SBA offers loan guarantee programs and other financial assistance to the small business owner. If you are eligible for an SBA guarantee program, your bank will be much more likely to provide financing. The SBA reduces risk to lenders by guaranteeing major portions of loans made to small businesses. This enables the lenders to provide financing to small businesses when funding is otherwise unavailable on reasonable terms.

When a small business applies to a bank or other lending institution for a loan, the lender reviews the application and decides if it merits a loan on its own or if it requires additional support in the form of an SBA guaranty. The lender then requests SBA backing on the loan. In guaranteeing the loan, the SBA assures the lender that, in the event the borrower does not repay the loan, the government will reimburse the lending institution for a portion of its loss. By providing this guaranty, the SBA is able to help tens of thousands of small businesses every year get financing they would not otherwise obtain.

The SBA 7(a) Loan Guaranty Program

The 7(a) Loan Guaranty Program is the SBA's primary loan program. The eligibility requirements and credit criteria of the program are very broad in order to accommodate a wide range of financing needs. To qualify for an SBA guaranty, a small business must meet the 7(a) criteria, and the lender must certify that it could not provide funding on reasonable terms except with an SBA guaranty. The SBA can then guarantee as much as 85 percent on loans of up to $150,000 and 75 percent on loans of more than $150,000. In most cases, the maximum guaranty is $1 million. Exceptions are the International Trade, and 504 loan programs, which have higher loan limits. The maximum total loan size under the 7(a) program is $2 million.

The Loan Process

To begin the SBA loan process, you must submit a loan application to a lender for initial review, as discussed above. If the lender approves the loan subject to an SBA guaranty, a copy of the application and a credit analysis are forwarded by the lender to the nearest SBA office. After SBA approval, the lending institution closes the loan and disburses the funds. You make monthly loan payments directly to the lender. As with any loan, you are responsible for repaying the full amount of the loan. There are no balloon payments, prepayment penalties, application fees or points permitted with 7(a) loans. Repayment plans may be tailored to each business.

A sample Application for an SBA Business Loan (SBA Form 4) is set forth at Appendix 16.

Use of Loan Proceeds

You can use a 7(a) loan to: (1) expand or renovate facilities; (2) purchase machinery, equipment, fixtures and leasehold improvements; (3) finance receivables and augment working capital; (4) refinance existing debt with compelling reason; (5) finance seasonal lines of credit; (6) construct commercial buildings; and/or (7) purchase land or buildings.

Terms, Interest Rates and Fees

The length of time for repayment depends on the use of the proceeds and the ability of your business to repay, which is usually five to 10 years for working capital, and up to 25 years for fixed assets such as the purchase or major renovation of real estate or purchase of equipment. However, the term cannot exceed the useful life of the equipment.

Both fixed and variable interest rates are available. Rates are pegged at no more than 2.25 percent over the lowest prime rate for loans with maturities of less than seven years and up to 2.75 percent for seven years or longer. For loans under $50,000, rates may be slightly higher.

The SBA charges the lender a nominal fee to provide a guaranty, and the lender may pass this charge on to you. The fee is based on the maturity of the loan and the dollar amount that the SBA guarantees. On any loan with a maturity of one year or less, the fee is just 0.25 percent of the guaranteed portion of the loan.

On loans with maturities of more than one year where the portion that the SBA guarantees is $150,000 or less, the guaranty fee is 2 percent of the guaranteed portion. On loans with maturities of more than one year, where the SBA's portion exceeds $150,000 but not more than $700,000, the guaranty fee is 3 percent, and it is 3.5 percent on loans over $700,000.

Collateral

You must pledge sufficient assets, to the extent that they are reasonably available, to adequately secure the loan. Personal guarantees are required from all principal owners of the business. Liens on personal assets of the principals may be required. However, in most cases a loan will not be declined where insufficient collateral is the only unfavorable factor.

Eligibility

In order to be eligible for the SBA loan, your business generally must be operated for profit and fall within the size standards set by the SBA. The SBA determines if the business qualifies as a small business based on the average number of employees during the preceding 12 months, or on sales averaged over the previous three years. Loans cannot be made to businesses engaged in speculation or investment.

Maximum Size Standards

In order to qualify for an SBA loan, your business must not exceed the SBA maximum size standards, as follows:

Manufacturing—500 to 1,500 employees

Wholesaling—100 employees

Services—Annual receipts from $2.5 million to $21.5 million

Retailing—Annual receipts from $5 million to $21 million

General Construction—Annual receipts from $13.5 million to $17 million

Special Trade Construction—Annual receipts not to exceed $7 million

Agriculture—Annual receipts from $0.5 million to $9 million

The SBAExpress Loan Program

The SBAExpress Loan Program provides loans in amounts up to $350,000. The program authorizes SBA preferred lenders to use mostly their own forms, analyses and procedures to process, service and liquidate SBA guaranteed loans. The SBA guarantees up to 50 percent of an SBAExpress loan. Loans under $25,000 do not require collateral. Like most 7(a) loans, maturities are usually five to seven years for working capital and up to 25 years for real estate or equipment. Revolving lines of credit are allowed for a maximum of five years.

The SBA Export Working Capital Program

The SBA Export Working Capital Program is a line of credit for financing foreign accounts receivable. It is a transaction-based program and can be revolving or non-revolving. The SBA provides a 90 percent guarantee to the lender. The business must have been in operation for at least 12 months prior to the application, and the proceeds can be used to finance materials and labor needed to manufacture or purchase goods and services for sale in foreign markets, including such items as consulting services, overseas travel to establish a market, and participation at trade shows. Funds cannot be used to refinance existing debt or purchase fixed assets. The maturity is generally 12 months or less but can be renewed up to a total of 36 months.

The SBA International Trade Loan Program

The SBA International Trade Loan Program provides short term and long term financing to small businesses that are engaged in international trade, preparing to engage in international trade, or adversely affected by competition from imports. The SBA can guarantee up to $1.25 million for a combination of fixed asset financing and permanent working capital.

The SBA 504 Loan Program

The SBA 504 loan program is the SBA's economic development instrument that supports American small business growth and helps communities through business expansion and job creation. This loan program provides long term, fixed rate, subordinate mortgage financing for acquisition and/or renovation of capital assets including land, buildings and equipment. Virtually all types of for-profit small businesses are eligible for this program. The SBA 504 loan is distinguished from other SBA loan programs as follows:

1. There is a lower down payment;

2. There is a fixed interest rate;

3. The rate is usually below market rate;

4. All project costs can be financed, including: (1) acquisition costs, such as land and building, land and construction of building, renovations, machinery and equipment; (2) soft costs such as title insurance, legal, appraisal, environmental and bridge loan fees; and (3) closing costs.

5. The collateral is typically the assets financed; and

6. The loan is long term, e.g., real estate loans have a 20-year term, and heavy equipment loans have a 10-20 year term.

Eligibility

Businesses eligible for an SBA 504 loan must be:

1. A small business with a net worth under $6 million and net profit after taxes under $2 million, or the business must meet other SBA size standards.

2. Organized as a for profit business.

3. Any type of business, including retail, service, wholesale or manufacturing.

The SBA 7(M) Microloan Program

The SBA 7(M) Microloan Program loans are provided directly by a network of intermediaries approved by the SBA for the purpose of making microloans—i.e., those ranging from $500 up to $35,000—to small businesses for the purchase of machinery, equipment, furniture, fixtures, inventory and also for working capital. These intermediaries also provide technical and management assistance to the owners. Most small businesses that are unable to obtain funding through conventional sources or the other SBA guaranteed loan programs should contact the microloan lenders in their area.

SOURCES OF EQUITY CAPITAL

As set forth below, there are a variety of alternatives to bank financing for small businesses, especially business start-ups.

Individual Investors

You may be able to raise money by bringing in investors with whom you will share the profits, if any, from your business. Such investors can be known individuals, such as relatives, friends and business associates, and may also include unknown investors, such as ex-entrepreneurs and wealthy business people, who have money to invest. Like venture capital companies, private investors often desire to take an active control in the business.

Venture Capital Companies

Another source of funding for small businesses—usually on a short-term basis—is a venture capital company. Venture capital companies are in the business of taking risks in return for larger returns, thus they will generally want to take an active role in your business. You may obtain information on venture capital from the SBA, as well as from your investment adviser, banker, lawyer and accountant.

Small Business Investment Companies

The Small Business Investment Company Program fills the gap between the availability of venture capital and the needs of small businesses that are either starting or growing. SBICs are privately owned and managed investment firms that are licensed and regulated by the SBA. SBICs generally raise their investment funds by borrowing from the federal government or banks. SBICs make capital available to small businesses through investments.

SBICs are for profit firms whose incentive is to share in the success of a small business. In addition to equity capital, SBICs provide long term loans, debt equity investments, and management assistance. The SBIC Program provides funding to all types of manufacturing and service industries. Some investment companies specialize in certain fields, while others seek out small businesses with new products or services because of the strong growth potential. Most, however, consider a wide variety of investment opportunities.

Although SBICs are more willing to take risks on new businesses, they are profit-motivated organizations and, therefore, will closely examine the profit potential of your business.

CHAPTER 8:
LICENSES, PERMITS, REGULATIONS AND INSURANCE

IN GENERAL

Even though your new business may start out small, it is still subject to government regulations. It is important to comply with any local, state and/or federal rules that may apply to your business. Regulations vary by industry so you should carefully investigate those laws that affect your particular type of business. For example, if your business deals with food preparation, most likely there are certain health department regulations that must be followed. Compliance is important to avoid penalties, fines and/or revocation of your business license.

LOCAL LICENSES AND PERMITS

As set forth below, in order to operate your business, you will likely need to obtain local licenses and/or permits to comply with your town, city, and county regulations. Information on licensing and permit requirements for your business may be obtained from city and county offices, including:

1. The city and/or county clerk's office;

2. The building and safety department;

3. The health department, e.g., for information about permits and regulations if your business involves food preparation;

4. The planning or zoning department;

5. The tax assessor office, e.g., for information about local taxes on property, fixtures, equipment, inventory, and income or gross receipts;

6. The police and fire departments, e.g., for information on combustible materials used or stored on your business premises, and crowd control and safe exit strategies from your premises.

7. The public works department.

Business Licenses

In most locations, every business must apply for a basic business license, sometimes called a tax registration certificate. You usually get the business license from your city or county. However, in addition to a business license, you will likely need other permits and licenses in order to comply with the many regulatory requirements that apply to small businesses.

Zoning Permits

Before signing your lease, make sure the space you plan to occupy is properly zoned for the type of business you have chosen. If not, you cannot operate your business legally in that location unless the local zoning board grants you a variance.

In addition, if you are operating your business out of your home, you may need a special permit. For example, if you live in an area designated as residential, as opposed to agricultural, commercial, or industrial, you must determine whether there are any restrictions or prohibitions on home-based businesses in the zoning regulations. If there are restrictions, try to adapt your business to comply with them, if at all possible. If home-based businesses are prohibited, however, you must apply for a variance or permit to operate the business.

Zoning laws may also regulate (1) off-street parking; (2) water and air quality; (3) waste disposal; and (4) the size, construction, and placement of signs advertising your business.

Building Permits

If you are locating your business in a new building, you may need to apply for a certificate of occupancy. If you plan on remodeling the space to suit the needs of your business—e.g., knocking down walls or expanding bathroom facilities—you may also need a building permit; therefore, you should check with the local building department before you begin renovation. You may also need separate permits for electrical, plumbing, heating, and ventilating work.

STATE LICENSES AND PERMITS

A business license is the main document required for tax purposes and conducting other basic business functions.

Occupations and Professions

State licenses are frequently required for certain occupations and professions, including cosmetologists; real estate brokers and agents; security guards; private investigators; accountants; barbers; construction contractors, physicians; appraisers; and lawyers, etc. In order to determine which occupations and professions are licensed by your state, you should always check with your state licensing authorities.

Licenses Based on Products Sold

Some state licensing requirements are based on the product sold. Depending on the business you choose, you may be required to obtain a state license for certain business operations. For example, a restaurant will require a liquor license to serve alcohol, and a convenience store must obtain a license to sell lottery tickets.

You should check with your state to determine the type of license you will need to operate your business. Many states have established small business assistance agencies to help small businesses comply with state requirements.

A directory of state websites offering business license information is set forth at Appendix 17.

Sales and Use Tax Permit

If your business involves selling goods, you will have to apply for a sales and use tax permit in order to collect sales tax from your customers. The sales tax collected is then paid to the state. The amount of sales tax varies depending on the state.

A sample application for a Sales and Use Tax Permit is set forth at Appendix 19.

Environmental Permits

The government monitors those businesses that may contaminate the environment. You may need a special permit if any of the following apply to your business:

1. Your equipment vents emissions into the air;

2. You need to discharge or store waste water; or

3. Your business involves or produces hazardous wastes.

Environmental regulations are not limited to manufacturing companies. Small businesses, such as dry cleaners and photo processors use dangerous metals and chemicals and are required to dispose of these materials safely and properly.

FEDERAL LICENSES AND PERMITS

Government-Regulated Businesses

Businesses that are highly regulated by the government generally require federal licensing, e.g., gun shops, pharmaceutical companies, investment brokers, etc. An example of a business that would be subject to federal licensing is an investment firm, which would be governed by the Securities and Exchange Commission (SEC).

Federal Securities Registration

If you will be sharing ownership with people who will not be actively working in the business, you may need to comply with federal securities laws. Securities laws are meant to protect investors from unscrupulous business owners. They require businesses to register the sale of certain kinds of ownership interests with the federal Securities and Exchange Commission (SEC). The registration process may be time consuming and costly.

Fortunately, many small business are eligible for an exemption from filing. For example, if you and your associates are setting up a business that you'll actively manage, you will qualify for an exemption and will not have to file any paperwork. Further information about federal SEC exemptions for small businesses may be obtained from the SEC website (http://www.sec.gov/smallbus/).

REGULATIONS GOVERNING EMPLOYERS

If your LLC has employees, there are a number of regulations governing the employer/employee relationship that must be followed, and records that must be kept, as discussed below.

The Employer Identification Number

An Employer Identification Number (EIN) identifies your business, similar to the way a social security number identifies an individual. Any business that has employees is required to have an EIN.

Although an individual owner may not be required to obtain an EIN in order to do business, there are advantages to having one. For example, it is preferable to give out your EIN when carrying out business transactions instead of your social security number, which you may want to safeguard. In addition, having an EIN for your business lends more credibility to your business.

You can apply for an EIN from the Internal Revenue Service by phone, fax, mail or online. There is no application fee.

An application for an Employer Identification Number (IRS Form SS-4) is set forth at Appendix 19.

Employment Eligibility Verification Records

The employer sanction provision of the Immigration Reform and Control Act of 1990 (IRCA) is concerned with the hiring of undocumented workers. Under this provision, employers must complete Form I-9, which is used to verify the employment eligibility and identity of employees. The I-9 form must be completed and retained by the employer for any employees hired after November 6, 1986. The employer must file the I-9 form within three days from the hiring date. An employer who does not file the I-9 form is also subject to penalties ranging up to $1,000 per employee.

Payroll Records

As set forth below, employers are required to withhold taxes and other deductions from their employees' salaries, make periodic deposits, and file quarterly payroll tax returns.

Federal Income Tax

Federal income tax is money withheld from an employee's earnings based on gross income, number of dependents, marital status, etc.

Federal Unemployment Tax

Federal unemployment taxes are employer-paid taxes.

State Income Tax

Approximately 41 states require the employer to withhold state income tax.

State Unemployment Insurance Tax

State Unemployment Insurance Tax is determined and controlled by the employer and is determined by the company's own unemployment experience.

State Disability Insurance

State Disability Insurance is assessed on employees by some states, and is determined by setting a maximum withholding amount and/or a wage base.

Social Security

Social Security tax is paid by both the employer and employee. The employer is responsible for collection and payment of the employee's contribution.

Medicare

Medicare is collected on the basis of a percentage of the first $135,000 of income.

Department of Labor Records

The Department of Labor (DOL) oversees and administers many programs and statutory schemes concerning employee-related issues, the most well known of which are the Equal Employment Opportunity Act (EEOA), the Fair Labor Standards Act (FLSA), and the Employee Retirement Income Security Act (ERISA). To comply with many of the DOL regulations, employers are required to maintain on file numerous forms concerning their employees.

Occupational Safety and Health Administration Records

Employers are responsible for maintaining a safe and healthy workplace for their employees. This requirement is overseen by The Occupational Safety and Health Administration (OSHA). Under the Occupational Safety and Health Act, employers are required to report to OSHA concerning compliance with various prescribed standards of safety and health, entailing additional paperwork for the small business owner.

Although the OSHA records are relatively simple, they are quite important. The required self-reporting documents include a summary and log of occupational injuries and illnesses, which must be filed annually, and a supplemental report describing each incident in detail.

PRODUCT TESTING RECORDS

If you are in the business of manufacturing and distributing products, you must be concerned with keeping records on testing procedures and outcomes.

TAX RECORDS

As you probably already know from your experience as an individual taxpayer, you cannot avoid the taxing authorities. The Internal Revenue Service (IRS), as well as many of the state taxing authorities, require a variety of forms to be filled out and submitted on a timely basis. The consequences of not properly filing the required paperwork with the federal and state taxing authorities can be costly.

UCC BAR CODES

The Uniform Code Council, Inc., a nongovernmental agency, assigns a manufacturer's ID code for the purposes of bar coding. Many stores require bar coding on the packaged products they sell. For additional information concerning a bar code for your small business, contact:

The Uniform Code Council, Inc.
P.O. Box 1244
Dayton, Ohio 45401
Telephone: 513-435-3870.

INSURANCE RECORDS

When starting a business, it is important to meet with an insurance agent who is knowledgeable about small business insurance needs. It is important to make sure you have adequate insurance coverage for the variety of risks involved in operating a small business. There are insurance policies available that are specifically designed to cover small businesses.

In addition, your other business relationships may require you to maintain certain types of insurance coverage. For example, if you lease your office space, your landlord will usually require you to produce a certificate of insurance.

Depending on the nature of your business, there will be certain risks for which it would be wise to obtain insurance. Some of the types of business-related insurance that may be considered are discussed below.

Automobile Insurance

Any vehicle owned by your business should be insured for both liability and replacement purposes. Fleet policy insurance is a type of blanket policy that covers a number of vehicles owned by the same business.

Business Interruption Insurance

Business interruption insurance is designed to cover certain specified expenses of a business while operations have been stopped due to some unforeseen situation. For example, if your business premises are damaged or destroyed by a fire, earthquake, flood, or some other unforeseen reason, certain expenses still need to be paid. These expenses may include employee payroll, taxes, utilities, and other expenses of upkeep during the time your business is being rebuilt.

Business Property Insurance

A business property policy would be required if you own the building in which your business is located. If you lease your premises, your landlord is required to provide this coverage. Your business personal property may also be covered under the policy, including your desks, chairs and equipment, etc.

Catastrophe Insurance

You should insure your premises, and your inventory, against such catastrophes as floods, fires, and earthquakes, or face a total loss should one of these events occur and destroy everything. Each such catastrophe is generally covered under its own policy, e.g., fire insurance, flood insurance, etc.

Crime Insurance

Crime insurance protects the insured from losses incurred as a result of burglary and robbery. Insurance premiums for crime insurance can be reduced if you maintain an alarm system for your business. If your business is located in a high crime area, depending on the state in which you live, you may be eligible for federal crime insurance, administered by the Federal Insurance Administration, which is a division of the Department of Housing and Urban Development (HUD).

Commercial Insurance

Commercial insurance protects and compensates parties to commercial contracts in the case of a breach of contractual obligations on the part of one of the parties.

Employer Liability Insurance

Employer liability insurance protects the employer against claims made by, or on behalf of, employees who are injured or killed during the course of employment, where such claims are not covered by worker compensation insurance.

Employment Practices Liability Coverage

Employment Practices Liability (EPL) insurance is a policy that covers risks that are not routinely covered under most business policies, such as lawsuits alleging wrongful termination or sexual harassment. This type of coverage becomes more important as the size of your business increases.

Employer-Provided Insurance

There are certain types of insurance applicable to the employer/employee relationship that an employer may be legally required to offer—or may voluntarily offer—its employees, as explained below.

Group Term Life Insurance

Group term life insurance is provided by an employer for a group of employees. The employee does not pay taxes on the premiums paid by the employer. There is no cash value to a group life term insurance policy.

Medical and Hospitalization Insurance

A medical and hospitalization insurance plan is one offered by an employer which covers certain specified illnesses and injuries suffered by employees. The plan can be contributory—wherein the employee contributes to the premium by deductions taken from his or her paycheck—or noncontributory.

Some of the other considerations in devising a medical and hospitalization plan include deductibles, coinsurance payments, benefit limits, and whether the covered persons will include the employee dependents as well as the employee. The health maintenance organization plan has become popular with both employers and employees, as its costs to the employer are lower than under a major medical policy, and it offers convenience to the employee, although it may take away the individual right to choose his or her own doctor without restrictions.

Unemployment Insurance

Unemployment insurance is a form of taxation collected from the business which is used to fund unemployment payments and benefits to former employees.

Workers Compensation Insurance

Workers compensation insurance compensates employees who are injured in the course of their employment, thereby protecting the employer from having to defend lawsuits brought by such employees. Employers who do not have worker compensation insurance when required by statute are directly liable to any injured employee.

Home Office Insurance

If you are establishing an office in your home, it is a good idea to contact your homeowners' insurance company to update your policy to include coverage for office equipment because this coverage is not automatically included in a standard homeowner's policy.

Key Man Life Insurance

Key man life insurance is purchased by the business on the life of an important or key officer or employee of the business. It is assumed that the business will suffer as a result of the loss of the particular individual thus entitling the business to the proceeds of such insurance upon his or her death.

Liability Insurance

Liability stemming from operation of your business can result in many ways. For example, if a customer is injured as a result of some dangerous or defective condition on your premises, e.g., because of a slip and fall, you may be liable for his or her injuries. In addition, if your employee, in the course of business, causes injury to a third party, you may be liable to the injured person. This could occur, for example, if your employee, while driving a company truck in the course of making a delivery, accidentally strikes a pedestrian. A comprehensive general liability policy can be purchased to cover all risks except those that are specifically enumerated as exclusions.

Excess liability coverage—i.e., liability limits over and above the maximum limits of your liability policy—is also available. Excess limits—e.g., in $500,000 increments—can usually be added to the underlying liability policy for an additional premium payment.

Malpractice Insurance

Malpractice insurance protects professionals from claims of professional malpractice brought against them. Malpractice insurance is available to many groups of professionals, such as doctors, lawyers, accountants, architects, engineers, and real estate agents.

Member Insurance

Partnership insurance is life insurance taken out on the lives of the members of a partnership or LLC, which is designed to enable the surviving member (or members) to buy out a deceased member estate. As your business grows this insurance can be increased.

Product Liability Insurance

If you are in the business of selling a certain product, you could be found liable to any person who is injured as a result of the use, or foreseeable misuse, of your product.

CHAPTER 9:
TAXATION ISSUES

IN GENERAL

A Limited Liability Company (LLC) is a fairly new entity created by state statute. The Internal Revenue Service (IRS) did not create a new tax classification for the LLC when it was created by the states. Instead, the IRS uses the tax entity classifications it has always had for business taxpayers: (1) corporation; (2) partnership; or (3) sole proprietor. An LLC is always classified by the IRS as one of these three types of taxable entities.

INCOME TAXES

Under federal tax regulations, a limited liability company (LLC) is permitted to elect its tax status for income tax purposes. A multi—member LLC can elect to be treated as either a partnership or a corporation, including an "S" corporation. A single—member LLC may elect to be classified as either a corporation or a sole proprietorship—referred to as a "disregarded entity." The LLC must make its tax status election by filing an Entity Classification Election on IRS Form 8832.

Default Rules

If the LLC does not elect its classification on IRS Form 8832, a default classification will apply. If the LLC has only one owner, it will automatically be treated as if it were a sole proprietorship (a "disregarded entity). If the LLC has two or more owners, for tax purposes, it will automatically be considered to be a partnership for tax purposes.

Single Member LLCs

As set forth above, when an LLC has only one member, the fact that it is an LLC is ignored or "disregarded" for the purpose of filing a federal tax return. However, this only applies for tax purposes. It doesn't change the fact that the business is legally a limited liability company. Single member LLCs are not permitted to file a partnership return.

If the only member of the LLC is an individual, the profits or losses of the LLC are reported on Schedule C and submitted with the owner's 1040 tax return. Even if you leave profits in the company's bank account at the end of the year, income tax must be paid on that money.

If the only member of the LLC is a corporation, the LLC income and expenses are reported on the corporation's return, usually IRS Form 1120 or 11210S.

Multiple Member LLCs

The IRS treats multiple member LLCs as partnerships for tax purposes. Like single member LLCs, multiple member LLCs do not pay taxes on business income. Most LLCs with more than one member file a partnership return (IRS Form 1065). This form is an informational return that the IRS reviews to make sure that LLC members are reporting their income correctly. The LLC must also provide each LLC member with a Schedule K-1, which breaks down each member's share of the LLC's profits and losses. Each member's share of profits or losses are reported on Schedule E and submitted with each member's 1040 tax return.

Reporting Losses

Many small businesses will report losses, especially in the early years, although this does not necessarily mean the business will not have a positive cash flow. Because the LLC is a pass—through entity, or conduit, for tax purposes, these losses can be passed on to the owners' personal tax returns, where they can offset, or shelter, other sources of taxable income.

For single—owner LLCs, the losses can offset any other type of income reported on your individual income tax return, including income earned by your spouse. For multiple—owner LLCs, the losses also can offset your other income, up to the amount you have invested in the business.

Special Situations

There are two common situations where unintentional errors may occur:

1. If you convert an existing business such as a corporation into an LLC, there may be tax implications, such as:

(a) The conversion may result in a taxable gain.

(b) Employment tax wage bases may be affected.

2. Special rules may apply when your LLC has an operating loss, as follows:

(a) The amount of loss you can deduct may be limited because of your limited liability for LLC debts.

(b) Passive activity loss limitations may restrict the amount of loss you can deduct.

If either of these situations applies to you, it is beyond the scope of this book, and professional advice may be needed. You can contact the IRS for more information at 1-800-829-1040 or go to their website at http://www.irs.gov/.

SELF-EMPLOYMENT TAXES

The LLC is not a taxpaying entity and, therefore, does not pay social security or any other employment taxes on the salary of the owner. The LLC owner is really self-employed, and the "salary" is only an owner's withdrawal from the business. However, the LLC owner must, on his or her personal income tax return (Form 1040), pay a "self-employment" tax, which is in reality the social security tax and the Medicare tax that would ordinarily be paid by the employer and the employee, which is further discussed below. If the LLC files as a partnership, the members pay self-employment tax on their share of partnership earnings. There is a special rule for members who are the equivalent of limited partners. They pay self-employment tax only if the LLC pays them for services.

EMPLOYMENT TAXES

Employment tax requirements apply to LLCs in much the same way as other types of businesses. If the LLC has employees, it is responsible for withholding and paying employment taxes, including, but not limited to: (1) federal income tax; (2) social security and Medicare taxes; and (3) federal unemployment tax.

A single member LLC may report and pay employment taxes in two ways: (1) using the name and EIN assigned to the LLC; or (2) using the name and EIN of the single member owner. In any event, the single member owner retains ultimate responsibility for collecting, reporting, and paying the employment taxes to the IRS.

As previously discussed, as an LLC member, your liability for LLC debts are limited by state law. However, you may be held personally liable in situations involving unpaid employee withholdings if you are found to be the person responsible for making the payments.

Thus, the IRS advises that the small business owner keep all records and employment taxes for at least four years. In addition, good recordkeeping helps you monitor the progress of your business, prepare your financial statements, keep track of deductible expenses, prepare your tax returns, and support items reported on your tax returns.

Federal Income Taxes/Social Security and Medicare Taxes

Your LLC must generally withhold federal income tax from your employee's wages. The IRS provides guidelines for employers to figure out how much to withhold from each wage payment in IRS Publication 15 (Employer's Tax Guide).

Social security and Medicare taxes pay for benefits that workers and families receive under the Federal Insurance Contributions Act (FICA). The LLC withholds part of these taxes from your employee's wages and the LLC pays a matching amount.

Federal income taxes, social security and Medicare taxes are reported on IRS Form 941, (Employer's Quarterly Federal Tax Return).

Federal Unemployment Tax (FUTA)

The federal unemployment tax is part of the federal and state program under the Federal Unemployment Tax Act (FUTA) that pays unemployment compensation to workers who lose their jobs. Your LLC reports and pays FUTA tax separately from social security and Medicare taxes and withheld income tax. The LLC pays FUTA tax only from the LLC's own funds. LLC employees do not pay this tax or have it withheld from their pay.

FUTA taxes are reported on IRS Form 940 (Employer's Annual Federal Unemployment Tax Return) or, if your LLC qualifies, you can use the simpler IRS Form 940-EZ.

Depositing Employment Taxes

In general, you must deposit the income tax withheld, and both the employer and employee social security and Medicare taxes, with the IRS. You can make your deposits either electronically, using the Electronic Federal Tax Payment System (EFTPS), or by taking your deposit and an IRS Form 8109-B (Federal Tax Deposit Coupon) to an authorized financial institution or a Federal Reserve bank serving your area.

STATE TAXES

State law imposes a tax based on the number of members of the LLC. Also, depending on the nature of the business it undertakes, the LLC may have to pay or collect sales taxes, withholding taxes and other taxes. A number of states have announced that they will follow the lead of the IRS with respect to LLCs in assessing state income taxes. Thus, the LLC automatically will be presumed to be a conduit for state tax purposes in these states, and no state corporate tax is imposed.

States that treat LLCs as a conduit for state taxes include:

Arizona

California

Maine

Maryland

Minnesota

New Jersey

Tennessee

Utah

While other states are likely to take the same lead, this is a fast—developing area of law. The reader is advised to contact their state tax department for information regarding state tax rules and regulations for LLCs.

SMALL BUSINESS EXPENSES

The following items are generally deductible as business expenses:

1. Vehicle Expenses—If you use your car for business or your business owns its own vehicle, you can deduct some of the related costs of operating and maintaining the vehicle. If you use your vehicle for both business and personal reasons, only the business use is deductible.

2. Business Operating Expenses—You may be able to deduct the cost of getting your business up and running, as well as ongoing operating expenses, such as rent, utilities, repairs, advertising, supplies, etc.

3. Training and Education Expenses—You can generally deduct training and educational expenses if they are related to your current business, and are necessary to maintain or improve your required skills in your present business.

4. Professional Fees—You can deduct the fees you pay tax professionals, accountants, attorneys or consultants in the year the charges were incurred.

5. Bad Debts—You can generally deduct bad debts, however, it depends on the type of product or service you offer. If you sell goods,

you can deduct the cost of goods that you sell for which you haven't received payment. However, if you offer services, you cannot deduct the time you spent with a client who then fails to pay you for your services.

6. Business Entertainment—If you pay for business entertainment, you may be able to deduct half of the expense if it is directly related or associated with your business, e.g., a business meeting at a restaurant.

7. Business Travel—If you travel for purposes related to your business, you may be able to deduct many of the expenses incurred on the trip, including airfare, transportation, lodging, meals, telephone and fax charges, etc.

8. Equipment—You can generally deduct the full cost of certain business equipment in the year you purchase the equipment.

9. Interest—If you use credit to finance business purchases, you can generally deduct the interest.

10. Charitable Contributions—Your business can make a charitable contribution and pass the deduction through to the members to be deducted on their personal income tax return.

There may be additional business expenses that will reduce your tax liability, therefore, you should contact the IRS or your state tax department and request information on allowable business deductions.

WORKING WITH YOUR SPOUSE

If you own a single-member LLC, you can run into liability if your spouse assists with the business on a regular basis. In general, a spouse can help out as long as their involvement is informal, infrequent and unpaid. However, if your spouse is paid, helps out regularly, and interacts with third parties on behalf of the LLC, you should add your spouse as an LLC member. Otherwise, you may be defeating the limited liability feature of the LLC.

There are several ways that the law might view your spouse's position in your LLC, and each has different consequences for both you and your spouse, as follows:

1. Agent—If your spouse is considered an agent of the LLC, the LLC would be responsible for any authorized actions of an agent. Nevertheless, the LLC structure would still protect your personal property from claims related to an agent's acts. The agent would not be personally liable for his or her actions, as long as they fell within the scope of his or her authority to act for the LLC.

2. Employee—If your spouse is considered an employee of the LLC, he or she would be personally liable only for certain extreme and unauthorized acts, such as assault or other criminal behavior. Again, the LLC structure would protect your personal property from liability for the acts of an employee, but if you failed to pay employment taxes, you could be subject to penalties. In addition, as with any employee, the LLC would be responsible for withholding taxes, reporting income, paying employment taxes, and providing workers' compensation and unemployment insurance, etc., thus defeating the simplicity of the single member LLC structure that has no employees.

3. Independent Contractor—If your spouse is considered an independent contractor, he or she could be held personally responsible for viritually all of his or her actions, thus, even though the LLC structure protects your personal property, your spouse's personal property, as well as any jointly owned property, would be at risk if he or she was successfully sued.

4. LLC General Partner—If your spouse is considered as a person who has entered into a general partnership with your LLC, your spouse would be personally liable for business debts, and again, your spouses' personal property and joint property would be at risk.

If you decide to add your spouse as an LLC member, you must follow the LLC operating agreement provision that govern how new members can be added to the LLC. If you do not have an operating agreement, you must follow any state default rules that apply for LLCs without operating agreements. If your LLC does have an operating agreement, you will also necessarily have to reflect any provisions relating to capital, profits, and voting interests of the LLC members.

CHAPTER 10:
DISSOLVING THE LLC

IN GENERAL

There may be a number of reasons you want to dissolve your LLC, e.g., it is not doing well financially, you have lost interest in the business, etc. Whatever your reasons are, you must still follow the legal rules for closing the business, as set forth below.

VOTE TO CLOSE THE BUSINESS

Unless you operate a single member LLC as a sole proprietorship, you must vote to close your LLC according to the provisions set forth in your LLC operating agreement. If you do not have an operating agreement, the default state rules for closing an LLC will apply. Under the default rules of many states, when one member wants to leave the LLC, the company dissolves. In that case, the LLC members must fulfill any remaining business obligations, pay off all debts, divide any assets and profits among themselves, and then decide whether they want to start a new LLC to continue the business with the remaining members.

If there is an existing LLC operating agreement, and one or more LLC members want to continue the LLC, they may be able to exercise the buyout provision of your LLC's operating agreement, if there is such a provision. A buyout agreement controls whether a departing member can force the other LLC members to buy out his or her interest in the business, and the price for the outgoing member's interest.

In any event, if the vote to dissolve the business is successful, the LLC must file the appropriate dissolution papers with the state office. All states have some form for dissolving or terminating an LLC, although it may be called by a different name, depending on the state, e.g., Certificate of Dissolution, Certificate of Termination, Articles of Dissolution, etc.

A sample Articles of Dissolution form for a limited liability company is set forth at Appendix 20.

CANCEL LICENSES AND PERMITS

You must cancel any business licenses and permits your LLC maintains by contacting the agency that issued the license or permit and notifying them that you are dissolving the business and want the license or permit cancelled. You should also request some confirmation of cancellation.

RESOLVE LLC DEBTS AND TAXES

You must make sure all of the debts, including taxes, of the LLC are paid. If your LLC has employees, make sure you file all of the final employment tax paperwork, and make any necessary tax deposits. Also, notify federal and state employment tax authorities that you are dissolving the LLC. If your business collected sales taxes pursuant to a sales and use tax permit, submit the final forms and any amounts due to the state office that collects your sales tax.

When income taxes are due, you have to file a final federal and state income tax return. For multiple member LLCs, check off the box on the federal return indicating that this will be your final return. If you are a single member LLC, stop filing Schedules C and SE with your Form 1040.

Before your last day in business, if you have employees, you should give them their final paychecks. Most states require employers to give employees their final paychecks on their last day of work or within a few days of closing the business. Also, some states require businesses to pay out accrued, unused vacation days at the same time. You should check your state law regarding these matters as they vary from state to state.

If your LLC owes any money to creditors, such as banks, utilities, suppliers, or landlords, you must pay those debts, in full, and ask for confirmation that such bills have been satisfied. You should also set aside some money to pay any debts that you may have forgotten about that show up after you have already closed the business.

On the other hand, if you are owed any money—i.e., if the LLC has accounts receivable—you should try to collect these debts before you close your business as it may be much harder to collect afterwards.

NOTIFY INTERESTED PARTIES

You should notify the creditors, customers and employees of the LLC that the business will be closing. Make sure that people who might need to get in touch with you after the business have closed have your contact information. Generally, you will need to notify: (1) your landlord, giving the required amount of notice; (2) suppliers; (3) service providers, such as utilities; (4) banks and financial institutions, e.g., to close your business bank account and pay off any balances on business loans or credit cards; (5) employees, giving at least two weeks' notice even if you are concerned that they will not return upon receiving notice of the business closing; and (6) customers.

CLOSING YOUR BUSINESS WHILE IN DEBT

If you are closing your business because you cannot financially support the business any longer, and you have many outstanding debts, you should first and foremost try to protect your personal assets.

Personal liability for business debts depends in large part on your business structure. As discussed, the LLC structure provides limited personal liability for business debts. However, there are some debts you cannot avoid. For example, the IRS will likely hold you personally responsible for payroll debts even if you operated as an LLC. In addition, if you personally guaranteed a business loan or credit card on behalf of the LLC, you will be personally liable for payment of the debt to the financial institution that extended the credit. If you pledged certain personal property as collateral, a creditor will be able to recover that property as well.

THE IRS BUSINESS CLOSING CHECKLIST

The IRS has prepared the following business closing checklist to assist small business owners who are planning to dissolve their business:

1. Make final federal tax deposits, either using the Electronic Federal Tax Paying System (EFTPS) or by filing IRS Form 8109-B.

2. File final quarterly or annual employment tax forms, as applicable:

(a) Employer's Annual Federal Unemployment (FUTA) Tax Return (IRS Form 940)

(b) Employer's Quarterly Federal Tax Return (IRS Form 941)

(c) Employer's Annual Tax Return for Agricultural Employees (IRS Form 943)

(d) Agricultural Employer's Record of Federal Tax Liability (IRS Form 943-A)

3. Issue final wage and withholding information to your employees on the IRS Form W-2 (Wage and Tax Statement)

4. Report information from W-2s issued on IRS Form W-3 (Transmittal of Income Tax and Statements)

5. File final tip income and allocated tips information return on IRS Form 8027 (Employer's Annual Information Return of Tip Income and Allocated Tips)

6. Report capital gains or losses, as applicable:

(a) U.S. Individual Income Tax Return (IRS Form 1040)

(b) U.S. Partnership Income Tax Return (IRS Form 1065)

(c) Capital Gains and Losses for Corporations (IRS Form 1120-Schedule D)

7. Report partner's/shareholder's shares, as applicable:

(a) Partner's Share of Income, Credits, Deductions, etc. (IRS Form 1065)

(b) Shareholder's Share of Income, Credits, Deductions, etc. (IRS Form 1120S-Schedule K-1)

8. File final employee pension/benefit plan on IRS Form 5500 (Annual Return/Report of Employee Benefit Plan)

9. Issue payment information to sub-contractors on IRS Form 100-MISC (Miscellaneous Income)

10. Report information from 1099s issued on IRS Form 1096 (Annual Summary and Transmittal of U.S. Information Return)

11. Report corporate dissolution or liquidation on IRS Form 966 (Corporate Dissolution or Liquidation)

12. Consider allowing S corporation election to terminate (IRS Form 1120S Instructions)

13. Report business asset sales on IRS Form 8594 (Asset Acquisition Statement)

14. Report the sale or exchange of property used in your trade or business on IRS Form 4797 (Sales of Business Property)

APPENDIX 1:
CERTIFICATE OF CONVERSATION

New York State
Department of State
Division of Corporations, State Records
and Uniform Commercial Code
Albany, NY 12231
www.dos.state.ny.us

CERTIFICATE OF CONVERSION
OF

(Insert name of Partnership/Limited Partnership) .
TO

(Insert name of Limited Liability Company)

Under Section 1006 of the Limited Liability Company Law

FIRST: The name of the limited liability company is: _____

_____ .

SECOND: The (partnership/limited partnership) was, in accordance with the provisions of the Limited Liability Company Law, duly converted to a limited liability company. (Please note: The conversion of a limited partnership to a limited liability company does not become effective until a certificate of cancellation is filed for the limited partnership. See LLCL §1006(f)(g) and PL §121-203.)

THIRD: The name of the (partnership/limited partnership) was:
_____ . In the case of a limited partnership, the date its initial certificate of limited partnership was filed by the Department of State is _____ .

FOURTH: The county within this state in which the office of the limited liability company is to be located is: _____ .

FIFTH: The Secretary of State is designated as the agent of the limited liability company upon whom process against it may be served. The address within or without this state to which the Secretary of State shall mail a copy of process against the limited liability company served upon him or her is: _____

_____

_____ .

X_____
(Signature)

_____
(Type or print name)

_____
(Title of signer)

CERTIFICATE OF CONVERSION
OF

TO

Under Section 1006 of the Limited Liability Company Law

Filed by: _____

_____

_____

NOTE: This form was prepared by the New York State Department of State for filing a certificate of conversion of a partnership or limited partnership to a newly formed limited liability company. It does not contain all optional provisions under the law. You are not required to use this form. You may draft your own form or use forms available at legal supply stores. The Department of State recommends that legal documents be prepared under the guidance of an attorney. The certificate must be submitted with a $200 filing fee made payable to the Department of State.

(For office use only)

APPENDIX 2:
APPLICATION FOR CERTIFICATE OF AUTHORITY

New York State
Department of State
Division of Corporations, State Records
and Uniform Commercial Code
41 State Street
Albany, NY 12231
www.dos.state.ny

APPLICATION FOR AUTHORITY
OF

(Insert name of Foreign Limited Liability Company)
Under Section 802 of the Limited Liability Company Law

FIRST: The name of the limited liability company is:_____
_____.

If the name does not contain a required word or abbreviation pursuant to Section 204 of the Limited Liability Company Law, the following word or abbreviation is added to the name for use in this state:

_____.

(Do not complete this section unless the limited liability company's true name is not available pursuant to §204 of the Limited Liability Company Law.) The fictitious name under which the limited liability company will do business in New York is:

_____.

SECOND: The jurisdiction of organization of the limited liability company is: _____.

. The date of its organization is: .

THIRD: The county within this state in which the office, or if more than one office, the principal office of the limited liability company is to be located is: _____.
(A county in New York State must be stated. Please note that the limited liability company is not required to have an actual physical office in this state.)

FOURTH: The Secretary of State is designated as agent of the limited liability company upon whom process against it may be served. The address within or without this state to which the Secretary of State shall mail a copy of any process served against him or her is:_____

_____.

FIFTH: (Complete the statement that applies)

The address of the office required to be maintained in the jurisdiction of its formation is: _____

If no office is required to be maintained in the jurisdiction of its formation, the address of the principal office of the limited liability company is: _____

SIXTH: The foreign limited liability company is in existence in its jurisdiction of formation at the time of filing of this application.

SEVENTH: The name and address of the Secretary of State or other authorized official in its jurisdiction of organization where a copy of its articles of organization is filed is: _____

X

(Signature)

_____
(Type or print name)

(Title or capacity of signer)

Please Note: A certificate of existence or, if no such certificate is issued by the jurisdiction of formation, a certified copy of the articles of organization of the limited liability company and all subsequent amendments therefore, or if no articles of organization have been filed, a certified copy of the certificate filed as its organizational base and all amendments thereto, **must be attached** to the application for authority when submitted for filing. If such certificate or certified copy is in a foreign language, a translation in English thereto under oath of the translator shall be attached.

APPLICATION FOR AUTHORITY

OF

_____

(Insert name of Foreign Limited Liability Company)

Under Section 802 of the Limited Liability Company Law

Filed by: _____

(Name)

_____

(Mailing address)

_____

(City, State and Zip code)

NOTE: This form was prepared by the New York State Department of State for filing an application for authority for a foreign limited liability company to conduct business in New York State. It does not contain all optional provisions under the law. You are not required to use this form. You may draft your own form or use forms available at legal supply stores. The Department of State recommends that legal documents be prepared under the guidance of an attorney. The certificate must be submitted with a $250 filing fee made payable to the Department of State.

(For office use only.)

APPENDIX 3:
CERTIFICATE OF REGISTRATION—LIMITED LIABILITY PARTNERSHIP (LLP)

New York State
Department of State
Division of Corporations, State Records & UCC
41 State Street
Albany, NY 12231
www.dos.state.ny.us

CERTIFICATE OF REGISTRATION
OF

(Insert Name of Domestic Registered Limited Liability Partnership)
Under Section 121-1500(a) of the Partnership Law

FIRST: The name of the registered limited liability partnership is:

SECOND: The address of the principal office of the partnership without limited partners is:

THIRD: The profession or professions to be practiced by such partnership without limited partners is:

The partnership is eligible to register as a registered limited liability partnership pursuant to Section 121-1500(a) of the Partnership Law.

FOURTH: The Secretary of State is designated as agent of the partnership without limited partners upon whom process against it may be served. The address to which the Secretary of State shall forward copies of any process against it or served upon it is:

FIFTH: The partnership without limited partners is filing this registration for status as a registered limited liability partnership.

(Signature of Partner)   *(Print or Type Name of Partner)*

DOS-1526 (Rev. 6/06)   -1-

How to Form a Limited Liability Company   **81**

CERTIFICATE OF REGISTRATION
OF

(Insert Name of Domestic Registered Limited Liability Partnership)
Under Section 121-1500(a) of the Partnership Law

Filed by:
(Name)

(Mailing address)

(City, State and Zip code)

NOTE: This form was prepared by the New York State Department of State for filing a certificate of registration for a domestic registered limited liability partnership. This form does not contain all optional provisions under the law. You are not required to use this form. You may draft your own form or use forms available at legal stationery stores. The Department of State recommends that legal documents be prepared under the guidance of an attorney. The certificate must be submitted with a $200 filing fee made payable to the Department of State.

Section 121-1500(p) of the Partnership Law requires a certified copy of the certificate of registration be filed with the licensing authority within 30 days after the filing with the Department of State. The fee for a certified copy is $10.

(For DOS Use Only)

How to Form a Limited Liability Company

APPENDIX 4:
CERTIFICATE OF PUBLICATION—LIMITED LIABILITY PARTNERSHIP (LLP)

New York State
Department of State
Division of Corporations, State Records
and Uniform Commercial Code
Albany, NY 12231
www.dos.state.ny.us

CERTIFICATE OF PUBLICATION
OF

(Name of Domestic Limited Liability Partnership)

Under Section 121-1500 of the Partnership Law

The undersigned is the   of
(Title)

(Name of Domestic Limited Liability Partnership)

If the name of the registered limited liability partnership has been changed, the name under which it was registered is: .

The certificate of registration was filed by the Department of State on: .

The published notices described in the annexed affidavits of publication contain all of the information required by Section 121-1500 of the Partnership Law.

The newspapers described in such affidavits of publication satisfy the requirements set forth in the Partnership Law and the designation made by the county clerk.

I certify the foregoing statements to be true under penalties of perjury.

(Date)

(Signature)

(Type or Print Name)

CERTIFICATE OF PUBLICATION

OF

_____
(Name of Domestic Limited Liability Partnership)

Under Section 121-1500 of the Partnership Law

Filed by: _____
      (Name)

      (Mailing Address)

      (City, State and Zip Code)

Note: This form was prepared by the New York State Department of State for filing a certificate of publication for a domestic limited liability partnership. You are not required to use this form. You may draft your own form or use forms available from legal stationery stores. The Department of State recommends that legal documents be prepared under the guidance of an attorney. This certificate of publication, with the affidavits of publication of the newspapers annexed thereto, must be submitted with a $50 filing fee payable to the Department of State.

For DOS Use Only

APPENDIX 5: CERTIFICATE OF WITHDRAWAL—LIMITED LIABILITY PARTNERSHIP (LLP)

New York State
Department of State
Division of Corporations, State Records & UCC
41 State Street
Albany, NY 12231
www.dos.state.ny.us

CERTIFICATE OF WITHDRAWAL
OF

(Insert Name of Domestic Registered Limited Liability Partnership)

Under Section 121-1500(f) of the Partnership Law

FIRST: The name of the registered limited liability partnership is:

If the name of the registered limited liability partnership has been changed, the name under which it was registered is:

SECOND: The date the certificate of registration was filed with the Department of State is:

THIRD: The address of the registered limited liability partnership's principal office is:

FOURTH: The registered limited liability partnership acknowledges that this withdrawal terminates its status as a registered limited liability partnership.

(Signature of Partner)

(Print or Type Name of Signer)

CERTIFICATE OF WITHDRAWAL
OF

(Insert Name of Domestic Registered Limited Liability Partnership)
Under Section 121-1500(f) of the Partnership Law

Filer's Name:

Address:

City, State and Zip Code:

Note: This form has been prepared by the New York State Department of State for filing a certificate of withdrawal for a domestic registered limited liability partnership. This form does not contain all optional provisions under the law. You are not required to use this form. You may draft your own form or use forms available at legal stationery stores. The Department of State recommends that legal documents be prepared under the guidance of an attorney. This certificate must be accompanied by a fee of $60 made payable to the Department of State.

(For DOS Use Only)

APPENDIX 6:
OFFICES OF THE STATE SECRETARIES OF STATE

STATE	ADDRESS	TELE-PHONE NUMBER	FAX NUMBER	EMAIL	WEBSITE
Alabama	P.O. Box 5616 Montgomery, Alabama 36103	334-242-5324	334-240-3138	n/a	http://www.sos.state.al.us
Alaska	333 W. Willoughby Ave 9th Floor Juneau, AK 99811	907-465-2530	907-465-3257	corporations@commerce.state.ak.us	http://www.commerce.state.ak.us
Arizona	1700 West Washington Street Phoenix, AZ 85007	602-542-3026	602-542-1575	n/a	http://www.azsos.gov
Arkansas	State Capitol Rm. 256 Little Rock, AR 72201	501-682-1010	n/a	business@sos.arkansas.gov	http://www.sosweb.state.ar.us

STATE	ADDRESS	TELE-PHONE NUMBER	FAX NUMBER	EMAIL	WEBSITE
California	1500 11th Street 3rd Floor Sacramento, CA 95814	916-657-5448	n/a	n/a	http://www.ss.ca.gov
Colorado	1700 Broadway Denver, CO 80290	303-894-2200	303-869-4860	administration@sos.state.co.us	http://www.sos.state.co.us
Connecticut	30 Trinity Street Hartford, CT 06106	860-509-6002	n/a	crd@po.state.ct.us	http://www.sots.ct.gov
Delaware	401 Federal St. Suite 4 Dover, DE 19901	302-739-3073	302-739-3812	dosdoc_web@state.de.us	http://corp.delaware.gov
District of Columbia	1350 Pennsylvania Ave. NW Room 419 Washington, DC 20004	202-727-6306	202-727-3582	os.eom@dc.gov	http://os.dc.gov
Florida	500 South Bronough St. Tallahassee, FL 32399	850-245-6500	850-245-6125	secretaryofstate@dos.state.fl.us	http://oss.dos.state.fl.us
Georgia	214 State Capitol Atlanta, GA 30334	404-656-2817	404-656-0513	n/a	http://www.sos.state.ga.us
Hawaii	250 So. Hotel Street Honolulu, HI 96813	808-586-2744	808-586-2377	director@dbedt.hawaii.gov	http://www.hawaii.gov/dbedt
Idaho	P.O. Box 83720 Boise, ID 83720	208-334-2300	n/a	n/a	http://www.idsos.state.id.us

STATE	ADDRESS	TELE-PHONE NUMBER	FAX NUMBER	EMAIL	WEBSITE
Illinois	213 State Capitol Springfield, IL 62706	800-252-8980	n/a	n/a	http://www.sos.state.il.us
Indiana	201 Statehouse Indianapolis, IN 46204	317-232-6576	n/a	n/a	http://www.in.gov/sos
Iowa	321 E. 12th St. Des Moines, IA 50319	515-281-5204	515-242-5953	sos@sos.state.ia.us	http://www.sos.state.ia.us
Kansas	120 SW 10th Ave. Topeka, KS 66612	785-296-4564	n/a	corp@kssos.org	http://www.kssos.org
Kentucky	700 Capital Avenue Suite 154 Frankfort, KY 40601	502-564-2848	502-564-4075	n/a	http://www.sos.ky.gov
Louisiana	P.O. Box 94125 Baton Rouge, LA 70804	225-925-4704	n/a	commercial@sos.louisiana.gov	http://www.sec.state.la.us
Maine	101 State House Station Augusta, ME 04333	207-624-7736	207-287-5874	n/a	http://www.maine.gov/sos
Maryland	State House Annapolis, MD 21401	410-974-5521	n/a	charterhelp@dat.state.md.us	http://www.dat.state.md.us
Massachusetts	One Ashburton Place Room 1611 Boston MA 02108	617-727-7030	617-742-4528	cis@sec.state.ma.us	http://www.sec.state.ma.us

STATE	ADDRESS	TELE-PHONE NUMBER	FAX NUMBER	EMAIL	WEBSITE
Michigan	Michigan Department of State Lansing, MI 48918	888-767-6424	n/a	secretary@michigan.gov	http://www.michigan.gov/sos
Minnesota	60 Empire Drive Suite 100 St. Paul, MN 55103	651-296-2803	651-297-7067	business.services@state.mn.us	http://www.sos.state.mn.us
Mississippi	700 North St. Jackson, MS 39202	601-359-1350	601-359-1499	n/a	http://www.sos.state.ms.us
Missouri	600 W. Main St. Room 322 Jefferson City, MO 65101	573-751-4153	n/a	n/a	http://www.sos.mo.gov
Montana	P.O. Box 202801 Helena, MT 59620	406-444-2034	406-444-3976	sosinfo@mt.gov	http://www.sos.state.mt.us
Nebraska	P.O. Box 94608 Lincoln, NE 68509	402-471-4079	402-471-3666	n/a	http://www.sos.state.ne.us
Nevada	101 N. Carson St. Carson City, NV 89701	775-684-5708	775-684-5724	sosmail@sos.nv.gov	http://www.sos.state.nv.us
New Hampshire	25 Capitol St. Room 341 Concord, NH 03301	603-271-3246	n/a	corporate@sos.state.nh.us	http://www.sos.nh.gov
New Jersey	P.O. Box 300 Trenton, NJ 08625	609-984-1900	609-292-7665	feedback@sos.state.nj.us	http://www.state.nj.us

STATE	ADDRESS	TELE-PHONE NUMBER	FAX NUMBER	EMAIL	WEBSITE
New Mexico	State Capitol North Annex Suite 300 Santa Fe, NM 87503	505-827-3600	505-827-3634	n/a	http://www.sos.state.nm.us
New York	41 State Street Albany, NY 12231	518-474-4752	518-474-4597	corpora-tions@dos.state.ny.us	http://www.dos.state.ny.us
North Carolina	2 South Salisbury St. Raleigh, NC 27601	919-807-2225	919-807-2039	n/a	http://www.secretary.state.nc.us
North Dakota	600 E. Boulevard Ave. Dept. 108 Bismarck, ND 58505	701-328-2900	701-328-2992	n/a	sos@nd.gov
Ohio	180 East Broad St. Columbus, OH 43215	614-466-2585	n/a	n/a	http://www.sos.state.oh.us
Oklahoma	2300 N. Lincoln Blvd. Room 101 Oklahoma City, OK 73105	405-521-3912	405-521-3771	n/a	http://www.sos.state.ok.us
Oregon	225 Capitol St. NE Salem, OR 97310	503-986-2200	503-986-6355	businessregistry.sos@state.or.us	http://www.sos.state.or.us
Pennsylvania	206 North Office Building Harrisburg, PA 17120	717-787-1057	717-783-2244	RA-CORPS@state.pa.us	http://www.dos.state.pa.us
Rhode Island	148 W. River St. Providence, RI 02904	401-222-3040	n/a	businessinfo@sec.state.ri.us	http://www.sec.state.ri.us

STATE	ADDRESS	TELE-PHONE NUMBER	FAX NUMBER	EMAIL	WEBSITE
South Carolina	P.O. Box 11350 Columbia, SC 29211	803-734-2158	803-734-1614	n/a	http://www.scsos.com
South Dakota	500 East Capitol Avenue Suite 204 Pierre, SD 57501	605-773-4845	605-773-4550	corpora-tions@state.sd.us	http://www.sdsos.gov
Tennessee	312 8th Ave. North 6th Fl. Snodgrass Tower Nashville, TN 37243	615-741-2286	n/a.	http://www.state.tn.us/sos	
Texas	1019 Brazos St. Austin, TX 78701	512-463-5555	n/a	corpinfo@sos.state.tx.us	http://www.state.tx.us
Utah	P.O. Box 142220 Salt Lake City, UT 84114	801-538-1041	801-538-1133	n/a	http://www.utah.gov
Vermont	81 River St. Montpelier, VT 05609	802-828-2386	802-828-2853	n/a	http://www.sec.state.vt.us
Virginia	111 East Broad St. 4th Fl. Richmond, VA 23219	804-786-2441	n/a	n/a	http://www.soc.state.va.us
Washington	801 Capitol Way South Olympia, WA 98504	360-753-7115	n/a	corps@secstate.wa.gov	http://www.secstate.wa.gov

How to Form a Limited Liability Company

STATE	ADDRESS	TELE-PHONE NUMBER	FAX NUMBER	EMAIL	WEBSITE
West Virginia	1900 Kanawha Blvd. East Bldg. 1 Suite 157-K Charleston, WV 25305	304-558-8000	304-558-8381	business@wvsos.com	http://www.wvsos.com
Wisconsin	30 W. Mifflin 10th Fl. Madison, WI 53702	608-266-3590	608-266-3159	statesec@sos.state.wi.us	http://www.sos.state.wi.us
Wyoming	200 West 24th St. Room 110 Cheyenne, WY 82002	307-777-7311	307-777-5339	corpora-tions@state.wy.us	http://soswy.state.wy.us

APPENDIX 7: APPLICATION FOR RESERVATION OF LLC NAME

Application for Reservation of Name
Under §205 of the Limited Liability Company Law

NYS Department of State
DIVISION OF CORPORATIONS, STATE RECORDS and UCC
41 State Street
Albany, NY 12231-0001

PLEASE TYPE OR PRINT

APPLICANT'S NAME AND STREET ADDRESS

NAME TO BE RESERVED

RESERVATION IS INTENDED FOR (CHECK ONE)

____ New domestic limited liability company (The Limited Liability Company Law requires that the name end with "Limited Liability Company," "LLC" or "L.L.C.")

New domestic professional service limited liability company (The name must end with "Professional Limited Liability Company" or "Limited Liability Company" or an abbreviation in §1212(b) of the Limited Liability Company Law.)

____ Existing foreign limited liability company intending to apply for authority to do business in New York State

____ Existing foreign professional service limited liability company intending to apply for authority to do business in New York State

Change of name of an existing domestic or an authorized foreign limited liability company

____ A person intending to form a foreign limited liability company which will apply for authority to do business in this state

____ Existing foreign limited liability company intending to apply for authority to do business in New York State whose name is not available for use in New York State and must use a fictitious name

Authorized foreign limited liability company intending to change its fictitious name under which it does business in this state

____ Authorized foreign limited liability company which has changed its name in its jurisdiction, such new name not being available for use in New York State

X_____

Signature of applicant, applicant's attorney or agent
(If attorney or agent, so specify)

Typed/printed name of signer

INSTRUCTIONS:
1. Upon filing this application, the name will be reserved for 60 days and a certificate of reservation will be issued.
2. The certificate of reservation, which will be in the form of a receipt, must be returned with and attached to the articles of organization, application for authority, certificate of amendment or with a cancellation of the reservation.
3. The name used must be the same as appears in the reservation.
4. A $20 fee payable to the Department of State must accompany this application.

NOTE: In all applications for existing domestic and foreign limited liability companies, the applicant must be the limited liability company.

APPENDIX 8:
ARTICLES OF ORGANIZATION—DOMESTIC
LIMITED LIABILITY COMPANY

ARTICLES OF ORGANIZATION
DOMESTIC LIMITED LIABILITY COMPANY
Office of the Secretary of the State
30 Trinity Street / P.O. Box 150470 / Hartford, CT 06115-0470 / Rev. 10/01/2004
See reverse for instructions

Space For Office Use Only	Filing Fee: $60.00

Please contact the Department of Revenue Services or your tax advisor as to any potential tax liability relating to your business.

1. NAME OF THE LIMITED LIABILITY COMPANY

2. NATURE OF BUSINESS TO BE TRANSACTED OR THE PURPOSES TO BE PROMOTED

3. PRINCIPAL OFFICE ADDRESS (See instructions for further details.)

4. APPOINTMENT OF STATUTORY AGENT FOR SERVICE OF PROCESS

Name of agent	Business address (P.O. Box is not acceptable)
	Residence address (P.O. Box is not acceptable)
	Acceptance of appointment
	Signature of agent

5. MANAGEMENT
(Place a check mark next to the following statement *only* if it applies)

____ The management of the limited liability company shall be vested in one or more managers.

6. MANAGER(S) OR MEMBER(S) INFORMATION

Name	Title	Business Address	Residence Address

7. EXECUTION

Print or type name of organizer	Signature

Reference an 8 ½ x 11 attachment if additional space is required

INSTRUCTIONS FOR COMPLETION OF THE ARTICLES OF ORGANIZATION
Domestic Limited Liability Company

Please contact the Department of Revenue Services or your tax advisor as to any potential tax liability relating to your business.

Instructions

1. NAME OF LIMITED LIABILITY COMPANY: Provide the name of the limited liability company. The name must include the business designation, i.e., Limited Liability Company, LLC, L.L.C., Limited Liability Co., Ltd. Liability Company, or Ltd. Liability Co.

2. NATURE OF BUSINESS: Provide a description of the business which the limited liability company will conduct. Note that it is sufficient to state that the purpose of the limited liability company is to engage in any lawful act or activity for which a limited liability company may be formed under the Connecticut Limited Liability Company Act.

3. PRINCIPAL OFFICE: Provide the complete address of the limited liability company's principal office. Include street number, street, city, state and postal code. A P.O. Box is acceptable only if provided as additional information.

4. APPOINTMENT OF STATUTORY AGENT: Provide the name of a statutory agent who agrees to receive any process notice or demand served upon the limited liability company. The agent may be a natural person who is a resident of Connecticut; a Connecticut corporation, limited liability company, limited liability partnership or statutory trust; or a foreign corporation, limited liability company, limited liability partnership or statutory trust, which has obtained a certificate of authority to transact business in Connecticut. A limited liability company may not be its own agent. If the agent is a natural person, such person must provide the complete street address of his or her business and residence. If the agent is an entity, it must provide the address of its principal office in the block designated for "Business address" and the person signing on its behalf must include his or her title on the signature line. **The agent must sign accepting the appointment.**

5. MANAGEMENT: Select the statement provided regarding the management of the limited liability company by placing a check before it only if the limited liability company is to be managed by one or more managers. If the limited liability company is to be managed by its members, leave the underlined space blank.

6. MEMBER OR MANAGER INFORMATION: The limited liability company must list the name, title, business and residence address of one manager or member of the limited liability company. Include street number, street, city, state and postal code.
    Note: P.O. Boxes are only acceptable as additional information.

7. EXECUTION: The organizer must print or type his or her full legal name and provide a signature. Note that the execution constitutes a statement made under the penalties of false statement that the information provided in the document is true.

How to Form a Limited Liability Company

APPENDIX 9:
ARTICLES OF ORGANIZATION—
PROFESSIONAL LIMITED
LIABILITY COMPANY (LLC)

New York State
Department of State
Division of Corporations, State Records
and Uniform Commercial Code
Albany, NY 12231
www.dos.state.ny.us

ARTICLES OF ORGANIZATION
OF

(Insert name of Professional Service Limited Liability Company)

Under Section 1203 of the Limited Liability Company Law

FIRST: The name of the professional service limited liability company is:

SECOND: The professional service limited liability company shall practice the profession(s) of:

THIRD: The county within this state in which the office of the professional service limited liability company is to be located is:

FOURTH: The Secretary of State is designated as agent of the professional service limited liability company upon whom process against it may be served. The address within or without this state to which the Secretary of State shall mail a copy of any process against the professional service limited liability company served upon him or her is: _____

FIFTH: The names and residence addresses of all individuals who are to be the original members and the original managers, if any, are:

(Attach the appropriate certificates from the licensing authority or a comparable authority of another state.)

SIXTH: *Complete parts 1 and 2 of this paragraph only if any of the original members and managers are domestic or foreign professional service corporations, domestic or foreign professional service limited liability companies, domestic or foreign registered limited liability partnerships or professional partnerships.*

1. The names of all domestic and foreign professional service corporations, domestic and foreign professional service limited liability companies, domestic and foreign registered limited liability partnerships and domestic and foreign professional partnerships who are to be original members and managers of this professional service limited liability company are:

_____

_____

(Attach the appropriate certificates of existence from the jurisdiction of formation, and, in the case of foreign entities, certificates of the New York State Secretary of State that such foreign entities are authorized to do business in New York.)

2. The names and residence addresses or, if none, the business address of all shareholders, directors, officers, members, managers or partners of all domestic and foreign professional service corporations, domestic and foreign professional service limited liability companies, domestic and foreign registered limited liability partnerships and domestic and foreign professional partnerships who are to be the original members or managers are:_____

_____

_____

(Attach the appropriate certificates from the licensing authority or a comparable authority of another state.)

X_____
(Signature of organizer)

_____
(Type or print name of organizer)

ARTICLES OF ORGANIZATION
OF

_____
(Insert name of Professional Service Limited Liability Company)
Under Section 1203 of the Limited Liability Company Law

Filed by:
(Name)

(Mailing address)

(City, State and Zip code)

NOTE: • This form was prepared by the New York State Department of State for filing basic articles of organization for a professional limited liability company. It does not contain all optional provisions under the law. You are not required to use this form. You may draft your own form or use forms available at legal supply stores. The Department of State recommends that legal documents be prepared under the guidance of an attorney. The certificate must be submitted with a $200 filing fee made payable to the Department of State.

• Section 1203(c)(1) requires a certified copy of the articles of organization be filed with the licensing authority within 30 days after the filing with the Department of State.

(For office use only.)

How to Form a Limited Liability Company

APPENDIX 10:
STATE LLC FILING FEES

STATE	LLC FILING FEE
Alabama	$40.00
Alaska	$250.00
Arizona	$50.00
Arkansas	$50.00
California	$70.00
Colorado	$50.00
Connecticut	$60.00
Delaware	$70.00
District of Columbia	N/A
Florida	$125.00
Georgia	$75.00
Hawaii	$100.00
Idaho	$100.00
Illinois	$500.00
Indiana	$90.00
Iowa	$50.00
Kansas	$150.00
Kentucky	$40.00
Louisiana	$60.00
Maine	$250 plus $105
Maryland	$50.00
Massachusetts	$500.00
Michigan	$50.00
Minnesota	$135.00
Mississippi	$50.00

STATE	LLC FILING FEE
Missouri	$100.00
Montana	$50.00
Nebraska	$100.00
Nevada	$125.00
New Hampshire	$85.00
New Jersey	$100.00
New Mexico	$50.00
New York	$200.00
North Carolina	$125.00
North Dakota	$125.00
Ohio	$85.00
Oklahoma	$100.00
Oregon	$40.00
Pennsylvania	N/A
Rhode Island	$150.00
South Carolina	$135.00
South Dakota	$50 min.
Tennessee	$300 min.
Texas	$200.00
Utah	$50.00
Vermont	$70.00
Virginia	$100.00
Washington	$175.00
West Virginia	N/A
Wisconsin	$130.00
Wyoming	$100.00

APPENDIX 11: CERTIFICATE OF PUBLICATION—DOMESTIC LLC

New York State
Department of State
Division of Corporations, State Records
and Uniform Commercial Code
Albany, NY 12231
www.dos.state.ny.us

CERTIFICATE OF PUBLICATION
OF

_____
(Name of Domestic Limited Liability Company)

Under Section 206 of the Limited Liability Company Law

The undersigned is the _____
(Title*)

of _____
(Name of Domestic Limited Liability Company)

If the name of the limited liability company has changed, the name under which it was organized is:

The articles of organization were filed by the Department of State on:

The published notices described in the annexed affidavits of publication contain all of the information required by Section 206 of the Limited Liability Company Law.

The newspapers described in such affidavits of publication satisfy the requirements set forth in the Limited Liability Company Law and the designation made by the county clerk.

I certify the foregoing statements to be true under penalties of perjury.

_____
(Date)

_____
(Signature)

_____
(Type or Print Name)

* This certificate must be signed by a member, manager, authorized person or attorney-in-fact. If the certificate is signed by an attorney-in-fact, include the name and title of the person for whom the attorney-in-fact is acting. (Example, John Smith, attorney-in-fact for Robert Johnson, member.)

CERTIFICATE OF PUBLICATION

OF

_____

(Name of Domestic Limited Liability Company)

Under Section 206 of the Limited Liability Company Law

Filed by: _____

(Name)

(Mailing Address)

(City, State and Zip Code)

Note: This form was prepared by the New York State Department of State for filing a certificate of publication for a domestic limited liability company. You are not required to use this form. You may draft your own form or use forms available from legal stationery stores. The Department of State recommends that legal documents be prepared under the guidance of an attorney. This certificate of publication, with the affidavits of publication of the newspapers annexed thereto, must be submitted with a $50 filing fee payable to the Department of State.

For DOS Use Only

Attach this page after the affidavits of publication.

APPENDIX 12: CERTIFICATE OF PUBLICATION— PROFESSIONAL SERVICES LLC

New York State
Department of State
Division of Corporations, State Records
and Uniform Commercial Code
Albany, NY 12231
www.dos.state.ny.us

CERTIFICATE OF PUBLICATION
OF

(Name of Domestic Professional Service Limited Liability Company)

Under Section 1203 of the Limited Liability Company Law

The undersigned is the

(Title*)

of

(Name of Domestic Professional Service Limited Liability Company)

If the name of the professional service limited liability company has changed, the name under which it was organized is:

The articles of organization were filed by the Department of State on:

The published notices described in the annexed affidavits of publication contain all of the information required by Section 1203 of the Limited Liability Company Law.

The newspapers described in such affidavits of publication satisfy the requirements set forth in the Limited Liability Company Law and the designation made by the county clerk.

I certify the foregoing statements to be true under penalties of perjury.

(Date)

(Signature)

(Type or Print Name)

---

* This certificate must be signed by a member, manager, authorized person or attorney-in-fact. If the certificate is signed by an attorney-in-fact, include the name and title of the person for whom the attorney-in-fact is acting. (Example, John Smith, attorney-in-fact for Robert Johnson, member.)

CERTIFICATE OF PUBLICATION

OF

(Name of Domestic Professional Service Limited Liability Company)

Under Section 1203 of the Limited Liability Company Law

Filed by:
(Name)

(Mailing Address)

(City, State and Zip Code)

Note: This form was prepared by the New York State Department of State for filing a certificate of publication for a domestic professional service limited liability company. You are not required to use this form. You may draft your own form or use forms available from legal stationery stores. The Department of State recommends that legal documents be prepared under the guidance of an attorney. This certificate of publication, with the affidavits of publication of the newspapers annexed thereto, must be submitted with a $50 filing fee payable to the Department of State.

For DOS Use Only

How to Form a Limited Liability Company

APPENDIX 13:
SAMPLE LLC OPERATING AGREEMENT

OPERATING AGREEMENT OF THE ABC BAKERY, LLC

Upon valuable consideration, the persons named below as "Members" hereby covenant and agree to be bound to the following as their LIMITED LIABILITY COMPANY OPERATING AGREEMENT dated this ___ day of _____, 2007 for THE ABC BAKERY, LLC, a limited liability company organized under the laws of the State of New York:

ARTICLE I: DEFINITIONS

As used in this Operating Agreement, the following terms are to have the meaning indicated below:

"LLC" means "Limited Liability Company" and "the LLC" means The ABC Bakery, LLC.

"LLC Ownership Percentage" means the percentage of the LLC owned by the member.

"State Law" means the laws of the State of New York.

ARTICLE II: GENERAL PROVISIONS

Section 2.1. Formation. Articles of Organization have already been filed with the appropriate state office. Members agree to execute any additional documents that may hereafter be required in connection with the formation, valid existence and dissolution of the LLC as a limited liability company under the laws of the State of New York.

Section 2.2. Company Name. The name of the LLC is "The ABC Bakery, LLC".

Section 2.3. Purpose of the LLC. The purpose of the LLC is to engage in any lawful act or activity for which a limited liability company may be organized under the laws of the State of New York.

Section 2.4. Place of Business. The business address of the LLC shall be determined by the Members.

Section 2.5. Registered Agent. The registered agent of the LLC shall be determined by the Members who shall also possess the power to remove or replace a currently serving LLC registered agent.

Section 2.6. Business Transactions of a Member with the Company. A Member may lend money to, borrow money from, act as surety, guarantor or endorser for, guarantee or assume one or more obligations of, provide collateral for, and transact other business with, the LLC and, subject to applicable law, shall have the same rights and obligations with respect to any such matter as a Person who is not a Member.

Section 2.7. Company Property. No real or other property of the LLC shall be deemed to be owned by any Member individually, but shall be owned by and title shall be vested solely in the LLC.

Section 2.8. No Term To Existence. The LLC's existence shall commence on the date of the filing of the Article of Organization with the appropriate state office and, thereafter, the LLC's existence shall continue in perpetuity without term.

Section 2.9. Accounting Period. The LLC year for financial statement and federal income tax purposes shall be a calendar year.

ARTICLE III: MEMBERS

Section 3.1 Members. The name, initial capital contribution, and LLC Ownership Percentage of the Members are set forth below, and may be amended from time to time to reflect the admission of new Members.

Member Name: John Smith

Initial Capital Contribution: $5,000

LLC Ownership Percentage (%): 50%

Member Name: Mary Jones

Initial Capital Contribution: $2,500

LLC Ownership Percentage (%): 25%

Member Name: Jack Johnson

Initial Capital Contribution: $2,500

LLC Ownership Percentage (%): 25%

Section 3.2. New Members. New members may be admitted to the LLC by a majority vote of the LLC members, each member having one vote per capita.

Section 3.3. No Liability of Members. All debts, obligations and liabilities of the LLC, whether arising in contract, tort or otherwise, shall be solely the debts, obligations and liabilities of the LLC, and no member shall be obligated personally for any such debt, obligation or liability of the LLC solely by reason of being a member.

Section 3.4. Access to LLC Records. Each LLC member shall have the right to inspect the books and records of the LLC during normal business hours after the giving reasonable notice to the LLC custodian of records.

Section 3.5. Actions by the Members. LLC members may take any action at a meeting in person, by proxy, or without a meeting by written resolution.

Section 3.6. Meetings. Meetings of LLC members may be conducted in person or by telephone conference.

Section 3.7. Voting Rights. Each LLC member shall be entitled to one vote per capita regardless of his or her LLC ownership percentage.

Section 3.8. Power to Bind the LLC. No LLC Member acting in his or her individual capacity shall have any authority to bind the LLC to any third party with respect to any matter.

ARTICLE IV: MANAGEMENT

Section 4.1. Management of the LLC. This LLC shall be managed by its members.

Section 4.2. Right to Appoint Managers. The LLC members reserve the right to appoint managers, who may also be members, at a later date.

ARTICLE V: CAPITAL STRUCTURE

Section 5.1. Intial Capital Contributions. Each Member has contributed an initial capital contribution to the LLC in the amount set forth below.

Member Name: John Smith

Initial Capital Contribution: $5,000

Member Name: Mary Jones

Initial Capital Contribution: $2,500

Member Name: Jack Johnson

Initial Capital Contribution: $2,500

Section 5.2. Additional Capital Contributions. Members may make additional capital contributions but shall not be required to do so.

Section 5.3. Raising Additional Capital. Additional capital may be raised by adding new Members to the LLC.

Section 5.4. Withdrawal Of Initial Capital Contributions. Except upon the dissolution or liquidation of the LLC as set forth herein, or the unanimous vote of all Members, no Member shall have the right to withdraw its initial capital contribution from the LLC.

Section 5.5. Maintenance of Capital Accounts. An individual capital account shall be maintained for each LLC Member consisting of: (1) the member's capital contributions; (2) increased by the member's share of LLC profits, (3) decreased by the member's share of LLC losses, and (4) further adjusted as required or allowed by the Internal Revenue Code.

Section 5.6. No interest shall be paid upon any member's capital account.

ARTICLE VI: ALLOCATIONS AND DISTRIBUTIONS

Section 6.1. Allocations to Capital Accounts. Except as may be required by the Internal Revenue Code, net profits, net losses, and other items of income, gain, loss, deduction and credit of the LLC shall be allocated among the Members in proportion to each Member's ownership percentage. For example, if a Member has an LLC Ownership Percentage of 50%, he or she shall be allocated 50% of all profits or losses for any given tax year.

Section 6.2. Tax Allocations. In the case of any special tax allocations allowed under the Internal Revenue Code, the method of allocation and formula determined by the Members shall be followed so long as it complies with state law and the Internal Revenue Code.

Section 6.3. Distributions. The LLC Members, by resolution issued pursuant to this agreement, may make distributions to the Members from time to time in amounts it deems appropriate; however, no distribution shall be declared or made if, after giving it effect, the LLC would not be able to pay its debts as they become due in the usual course of business or the LLC's total assets would be less than the sum of its total liabilities.

ARTICLE VII: OWNERSHIP TRANSFER UPON THE WITHDRAWAL, DEATH, OR REMOVAL OF AN LLC MEMBER

Section 7.1. Transfer of LLC Ownership. No Member shall have the right to sell, convey, assign, transfer, pledge, grant a security interest in or otherwise dispose of all or any part of its LLC ownership other than to another LLC Member.

Section 7.2. Withdrawal Of Member. The withdrawal of an LLC Member is subject to the following provisions:

(1) Members shall have the unilateral right to resign or withdraw at any time from the LLC upon thirty (30) days written notice to each of the other LLC Members;

(2) Upon withdrawal, the withdrawing Member shall receive, in exchange for his or her LLC ownership percentage, the withdrawal compensation amount to be paid within 60 days of the effective date of the Member's withdrawal;

(3) The "Withdrawal Compensation Amount" is defined herein as 100% of the withdrawing member's capital account;

(4) Any withdrawing LLC member possessing a negative capital account upon the effective date of withdrawal shall have a duty to repay the negative balance of his or her capital account to the LLC upon withdrawal.

(5) Upon withdrawal, the withdrawing Member shall have no continuing obligations to the LLC other than pursuant to state law, this operating agreement or any other applicable laws.

Section 7.3. Death Of Member. The death of an LLC Member shall trigger the following provisions:

(1) Upon the death of a Member, the remaining LLC members shall promptly prepare financial statements for the LLC as of the end of the month in which the Member died, which shall be the effective date of death for the deceased Member for accounting purposes under this operating agreement.

(2) The estate of the deceased Member shall receive the Death Compensation Amount to be paid within 60 days of the effective date of the Member's death.

(3) The "Death Compensation Amount" is defined herein as 100% of the deceased member's capital account;

Section 7.4. Removal Of Member. A Member may be involuntarily removed from the LLC subject to the following provisions:

(1) The Member may be removed if: (a) the Member is required to provide services to the LLC and said Member is not substantially performing the promised services; or (b) the Member has defaulted upon his or her obligations under this agreement to make capital contributions to the LLC.

(2) The removed Member shall receive in exchange for his or her LLC ownership percentage the Removal Compensation Amount to be paid within 60 days of the effective date of the Member's removal.

(3) The "Removal Compensation Amount" is defined herein as 100% of the removed member's capital account.

ARTICLE VIII: DISSOLUTION OF THE COMPANY

Section 8.1. Dissolution. Dissolution of the LLC is subject to the following provisions:

(1) A majority vote of the Members is required to dissolve the LLC;

(2) No other event, including but not limited to, the withdrawal, removal, death, insolvency, liquidation, dissolution, expulsion, bankruptcy, or physical or mental incapacity of any LLC Member, shall cause the existence of the LLC to terminate or dissolve.

ARTICLE IX: EXCULPATION OF LIABILITY/INDEMNIFICATION

Section 9.1. Exculpation of Liability. A person who is an LLC Member shall not be liable for the acts, debts or liabilities of the LLC to third parties, i.e., persons other than the LLC or LLC Members.

Section 9.2. Indemnification. The LLC shall indemnify any Member of the LLC who was or is a party or is threatened to be made a party to a potential, pending or completed action, suit or proceeding, whether civil, criminal, administrative, or investigative, and whether formal or informal, by reason of the fact that such person is or was a Member of the LLC. Indemnification shall be limited to expenses, including attorney's fees, judgments, penalties, fines, and amounts paid in settlement actually and reasonably incurred by such person in connection with the action, suit or proceeding, if, and only if, the person acted in good faith, with the care an ordinary prudent person in a like position would exercise under similar circumstances.

ARTICLE X: MISCELLANEOUS

Section 10.1 Amendment of Operating Agreement. This Agreement may be amended by, and only by, a written resolution setting forth in detail the amendment and signed by all LLC Members.

Section 10.2. Successors. This Agreement shall be binding upon all successors in interest of the Members that includes, but is not limited to, executors, personal representatives, estates, trustees, heirs, beneficiaries, assignees, nominees, and creditors of the Members.

Section 10.3. Counterparts. This Agreement may be executed in several counterparts with the same effect as if the parties executing the several counterparts had all executed one counterpart.

Section 10.4. Governing Law. This Agreement shall be governed by and construed in accordance with the laws of the State of New York. Each Member hereby submits to personal and subject matter jurisdiction in the State of New York of any dispute between or among the Members and the LLC.

Section 10.5. Severability. If it shall be determined by a court that any provision or wording of this Agreement shall be invalid or unenforceable under state or other applicable law, such invalidity or unenforceability shall not invalidate the entire Agreement.

IN WITNESS WHEREOF, the undersigned have duly executed this Operating Agreement as of the date first above written as Members:

Signature Line: [John Smith]

Signature Line: [Mary Jones]

Signature Line: [Jack Johnson]

APPENDIX 14:
SAMPLE LLC BUSINESS PLAN

COVER PAGE

The cover page should contain the basic information about your company, including the name, address and telephone number of the company, and the contact person. You can also include a space to input the name of the person to whom you are giving a copy of your business plan and the date sent.

PART 1: INVESTOR FUNDS

This section should discuss the type of investment being offered, and the total percentage of ownership that is being offered. Explain why the company is seeking additional financing, e.g., to increase manufacturing capabilities, to expand its market, etc., and show how those funds will be used. Include sections that explain the risks involved, and the potential return on the investment.

PART 2: ABOUT THE COMPANY

This section summarizes the background and goals of the company. Describe the historical background of your company, including the date of organization, legal structure, and the date and state in which the articles of organization were filed. Discuss the product or service, and the company's track record, if any, in the particular business. Explain why this company is expected to succeed.

PART 3: ABOUT THE PRODUCT (OR SERVICE)

This section should include a detailed description of the product or service, including the costs involved, such as the costs of research and development, manufacturing, and distribution. Also discuss your pricing plans, the sales projections, and potential profits. Compare and differentiate your product or service from those already available. If your product or service is unique, explain why. Include information concerning the legal status of your product, such as patent and trademark protection.

PART 4: THE MARKET

This section should discuss all aspects of the market for the product or service. Detail the overall size and nature of the market, as well as your targeted market segment. Provide hard statistical data that indicates a growing need for your particular product or service. Discuss why the product or service your company offers will be competitive in the market, and differentiate your product or service from those of other companies in the same type of business. Describe your marketing plan, including the established methods of advertising, distribution, and sales. If your product or service is unique, explain what needs it will fulfill and why it will succeed. In addition, discuss future growth and the possible crossover into new markets.

PART 5: COMPANY MANAGEMENT AND PERSONNEL

This section should list your company's management personnel and supporting staff. Discuss each manager's background, accomplishments and experience, and how they will contribute to the success of the company, and state the level of compensation. If any manager has had prior success in the particular business, point that out as well. This section should also include an organizational chart of the various departments of your company, the key support personnel in each department, and their job descriptions.

PART 6: OWNERSHIP AND CONTROL

This section should discuss ownership and control of the company. Discuss the principal's experience in the particular field and qualifications. If applicable, include a list of the LLC members of your company and how they acquired their equity.

PART 7: FINANCIAL ANALYSIS

This section should summarize the company's financial condition, including capital contributions and outstanding debt. Detail the prior use of funds, such as research and development, advertising, manufacturing and distribution costs, and working capital. Include documentation of past performance of the company.

PART 8: RISK ANALYSIS

This section should include an analysis of the risks, including the methods undertaken to reduce such risks. Outline and discuss various financial scenarios, including the worst-case and best-case scenarios.

PART 9: STRATEGIES, OBJECTIVES, AND GOALS

This section should discuss your operating plan, including your specific strategies, objectives, and short-term and long-term goals. Outline the objectives you wish to accomplish at various intervals—e.g., quarterly—and your ultimate goal. Include your financial projections for the next 5 years.

APPENDICES

The appendices may include copies of the LLC operating agreement, LLC member resumes, statistical data, financial tables, newspaper clippings, etc., which support the various parts of the plan.

APPENDIX 15:
PERSONAL FINANCIAL STATEMENT

OMB APPROVAL NO. 3245-0188
EXPIRATION DATE:3/31/2008

PERSONAL FINANCIAL STATEMENT

U.S. SMALL BUSINESS ADMINISTRATION

As of _____ , _____

Complete this form for: (1) each proprietor, or (2) each limited partner who owns 20% or more interest and each general partner, or (3) each stockholder owning 20% or more of voting stock, or (4) any person or entity providing a guaranty on the loan.

Name	Business Phone
Residence Address	Residence Phone
City, State, & Zip Code	

Business Name of Applicant/Borrower

ASSETS	(Omit Cents)	LIABILITIES	(Omit Cents)
Cash on hand & in Banks	$	Accounts Payable	$
Savings Accounts	$	Notes Payable to Banks and Others	$
IRA or Other Retirement Account	$	(Describe in Section 2)	
Accounts & Notes Receivable	$	Installment Account (Auto)	$
Life Insurance-Cash Surrender Value Only	$	Mo. Payments $	
(Complete Section 8)		Installment Account (Other)	$
Stocks and Bonds	$	Mo. Payments $	
(Describe in Section 3)		Loan on Life Insurance	$
Real Estate	$	Mortgages on Real Estate	$
(Describe in Section 4)		(Describe in Section 4)	
Automobile-Present Value	$	Unpaid Taxes	$
Other Personal Property	$	(Describe in Section 6)	
(Describe in Section 5)		Other Liabilities	$
Other Assets	$	(Describe in Section 7)	
(Describe in Section 5)		Total Liabilities	$
		Net Worth	$
Total	$	**Total**	$

Section 1. Source of Income		Contingent Liabilities	
Salary	$	As Endorser or Co-Maker	$
Net Investment Income	$	Legal Claims & Judgments	$
Real Estate Income	$	Provision for Federal Income Tax	$
Other Income (Describe below)*	$	Other Special Debt	$

Description of Other Income in Section 1.

*Alimony or child support payments need not be disclosed in "Other Income" unless it is desired to have such payments counted toward total income.

Section 2. Notes Payable to Banks and Others.   (Use attachments if necessary. Each attachment must be identified as a part of this statement and signed.)

Name and Address of Noteholder(s)	Original Balance	Current Balance	Payment Amount	Frequency (monthly, etc.)	How Secured or Endorsed Type of Collateral

SBA Form 413 (3-05) **Previous Editions Obsolete**

This form was electronically produced by Elite Federal Forms, Inc.

(tumble)

Section 3. Stocks and Bonds. (Use attachments if necessary. Each attachment must be identified as a part of this statement and signed).

Number of Shares	Name of Securities	Cost	Market Value Quotation/Exchange	Date of Quotation/Exchange	Total Value

Section 4. Real Estate Owned. (List each parcel separately. Use attachment if necessary. Each attachment must be identified as a part of this statement and signed.)

	Property A	Property B	Property C
Type of Property			
Address			
Date Purchased			
Original Cost			
Present Market Value			
Name & Address of Mortgage Holder			
Mortgage Account Number			
Mortgage Balance			
Amount of Payment per Month/Year			
Status of Mortgage			

Section 5. Other Personal Property and Other Assets. (Describe, and if any is pledged as security, state name and address of lien holder, amount of lien, terms of payment and if delinquent, describe delinquency)

Section 6.   Unpaid Taxes. (Describe in detail, as to type, to whom payable, when due, amount, and to what property, if any, a tax lien attaches.)

Section 7.   Other Liabilities. (Describe in detail.)

Section 8.   Life Insurance Held. (Give face amount and cash surrender value of policies - name of insurance company and beneficiaries)

I authorize SBA/Lender to make inquiries as necessary to verify the accuracy of the statements made and to determine my creditworthiness. I certify the above and the statements contained in the attachments are true and accurate as of the stated date(s). These statements are made for the purpose of either obtaining a loan or guaranteeing a loan. I understand FALSE statements may result in forfeiture of benefits and possible prosecution by the U.S. Attorney General (Reference 18 U.S.C. 1001).

Signature:	Date:	Social Security Number:
Signature:	Date:	Social Security Number:

PLEASE NOTE: The estimated average burden hours for the completion of this form is 1.5 hours per response. If you have questions or comments concerning this estimate or any other aspect of this information, please contact Chief, Administrative Branch, U.S. Small Business Administration, Washington, D.C. 20416, and Clearance Officer, Paper Reduction Project (3245-0188), Office of Management and Budget, Washington, D.C. 20503. **PLEASE DO NOT SEND FORMS TO OMB.**

APPENDIX 16:
SBA APPLICATION FOR BUSINESS LOAN

U. S. Small Business Administration
APPLICATION FOR BUSINESS LOAN

Individual	Full Address	

Name of Applicant Business	Tax I.D. No. or SSN

Full Street Address of Business	Tel. No. (inc. Area Code)

City	County	State	Zip	Number of Employees (including subsidiaries and affiliates)

Type of Business	Date Business Established	At Time of Application _____
		If Loan is Approved _____

Bank of Business Account and Address	Subsidiaries or Affiliates _____ (Separate for above)

Use of Proceeds: (Enter Gross Dollar Amounts Rounded to the Nearest Hundreds)	Loan Requested			Loan Request
Land Acquisition		Pay off SBA Loan		
New Construction/ Expansion Repair		Pay off Bank Loan (Non SBA Associated)*		
Acquisition and/or Repair of Machinery and Equipment		Other Debt Payment (Non SBA Associated)		
Inventory Purchase		All Other		
Working Capital (including Accounts Payable)		Total Loan Requested		
Acquisition of Existing Business		Term of Loan - (Requested Mat.)		_____ Yrs.

CURRENT AND PREVIOUS SBA AND OTHER GOVERNMENT DEBT: Complete the chart for the following: 1) SBA loan applications pending for the applicant or any of its affiliates; 2) Federal debt, including SBA, received by the applicant including loans that have been paid in full or charged off; 3) Federal debt (including student loans and disaster loans) borrowed by any principal of the applicant; 4) Federal debt borrowed by any other business currently or previously owned by any principal of the applicant. If there has been a loss to the government as a result of a charge off, compromise, or discharge due to bankruptcy for any of the listed debt, it must be identified below. LOSS is the outstanding principal balance of the loan that the government agency had to write off after all collection activities (including compromises) were finalized.

Name of Agency	Borrower's Name	Original Amount of Loan	Date of Application	Loan Status	Outstanding Balance	$ Amount of Loss to the Gov't.
Agency Loan #						
#		$			$	$
#		$			$	$

ASSISTANCE List below the name(s), occupation, and address of anyone (including the lender) who assisted in the preparation of this form and who received (or will receive) compensation from the applicant for this assistance. For any person listed, an SBA Form 159 must be completed by the applicant and listed person and submitted as part of the application. The lender must complete the "Lender's Certification" on any SBA Form 159 prior to the loan being approved.

Name and Occupation	Address	Total Fees Paid	Fees Due
Name and Occupation	Address	Total Fees Paid	Fees Due

Note: The estimated burden completing this form is 12.0 hours per response. You will not be required to respond to collection of information unless it displays a currently valid OMB approval number. Comments on the burden should be sent to U.S. Small Business Administration, Chief, AIB, 409 3rd St., S.W., Washington, DC. 20416 and Desk Office for Small Business Administration, Office of Management and Budget, New Executive Building, room 10202 Washington, D.C. 20503. OMB Approval (3245-0016). **PLEASE DO NOT SEND FORMS TO OMB. SUBMIT COMPLETED APPLICATION TO LENDER OF CHOICE.**

SBA Form 4 (2-05) Previous Edition Obsolete

Page 1

ALL EXHIBITS MUST BE SIGNED AND DATED BY PERSON SIGNING THIS FORM

BUSINESS INDEBTEDNESS: Furnish the following information on all outstanding installment debts, contracts, notes, and mortgages payable. Indicate by an asterisk (*) items to be paid by loan proceeds and reasons for paying them. (Present balance should agree with the latest balance sheet submitted).

To Whom Payable	Original Amount	Original Date	Present Balance	Rate of Interest	Maturity Date	Monthly Payment	Security	Current or Past Due
Acct. #	$		$			$		
Acct. #	$		$			$		
Acct. #	$		$			$		
Acct. #	$		$			$		
Acct. #	$		$			$		
Acct. #	$		$			$		
Acct. #	$		$			$		
Acct. #	$		$			$		
Acct. #	$		$			$		

MANAGEMENT (Proprietor, partners, officers, directors, all holders of outstanding stock –100% of ownership must be shown.) Use separate sheet if necessary.

Name and Social Security Number And Position/Title	Complete Address	% Owned	*Military Service From To	*Sex
			Service Disabled ☐	
Race *: Amer. Ind./Alaska Native ☐ Black/Afr.-Amer.☐Asian ☐ Native Haw./Pacific Islander ☐White/Cauc. ☐			Ethnicity *Hisp./Latino ☐ Not Hisp./Latino ☐	
			Service Disabled ☐	
Race *: Amer. Ind./Alaska Native ☐ Black/Afr.-Amer.☐Asian ☐ Native Haw./Pacific Islander ☐White/Cauc. ☐			Ethnicity *Hisp./Latino ☐ Not Hisp./Latino ☐	
			Service Disabled ☐	
Race *: Amer. Ind./Alaska Native ☐ Black/Afr.-Amer.☐Asian ☐ Native Haw./Pacific Islander ☐White/Cauc. ☐			Ethnicity *Hisp./Latino ☐ Not Hisp./Latino ☐	
			Service Disabled ☐	
Race *: Amer. Ind./Alaska Native ☐ Black/Afr.-Amer.☐Asian ☐ Native Haw./Pacific Islander ☐White/Cauc. ☐			Ethnicity *Hisp./Latino ☐ Not Hisp./Latino ☐	

*This data is collected for statistical purposes only. It has no bearing on the credit decision. Disclosure is voluntary. One or more boxes for race may be selected.

THE FOLLOWING EXHIBITS MUST BE COMPLETED WHERE APPLICABLE. ALL QUESTIONS ANSWERED ARE MADE A PART OF THE APPLICATION.

For Guaranty Loans please provide an original and one copy (Photocopy is Acceptable) of the Application Form and all Exhibits to the participating Lender. For Direct Loans submit one original copy of the application and Exhibits to SBA.

1.Submit SBA Form 912 (Statement of Personal History) for each type of individual that the Form 912 requires.

2. If your collateral consists of (A) Land and Building, (B) Machinery and Equipment, (C) Furniture and Fixtures, (D) Accounts Receivable, (E) Inventory, (F) Other, please provide an itemized list that contains serial and identification numbers for all articles that had an original value of greater than $5,000. Include a legal description of Real Estate offered as collateral. Label it Exhibit A.

3. Furnish a signed current personal balance sheet (SBA Form 413 may be used for this purpose) for each stockholder (with 20% or greater ownership), partner, officer, and owner. Include the assets and liabilities of the spouse and any close relatives living in the household. Also, include your Social Security Number. The date should be the same as the most recent business financial statement. Label it Exhibit B.

4. Include the financial statements listed below: a, b, c for the last three years; also a, b, c, and d as of the same date, - current within 90 days of filing the application; and statement e, if applicable. Label it Exhibit C (Contact SBA for a referral if assistance with preparation is wanted.) All information must be signed and dated.

a. Balance Sheet
b. Profit and Loss Statement (if not available, explain why and substitute Federal income tax forms)
c. Reconciliation of Net Worth
d. Aging of Accounts Receivable and Payable (summary)
e. Projection of earnings for at least one year where financial statements for the last three years are unavailable or when SBA requests them.

5. Provide a brief history of your company and a paragraph describing the expected benefits it will receive from the loan. Label it Exhibit D.

6. Provide a brief description similar to a resume of the education, technical and business background for all the people listed under Management. Label it Exhibit E.

How to Form a Limited Liability Company

7. Submit the name, addresses, tax I.D. number (EIN or SSN), and current personal balance sheet(s) of any co-signers and/or guarantors for the loan who are not otherwise affiliated with the business. Exhibit F.

8. Include a list of any machinery or equipment or other non-real estate assets to be purchased with loan proceeds and the cost of each item as quoted by the seller. Include the seller's name and address. Exhibit G.

9. Have you or any officer of your company ever been involved in bankruptcy or insolvency proceedings? If so, please provide the details as Exhibit H.
If none, check here: [ ]Yes [ ]No

10. Are you or your business involved in any pending lawsuits? If yes provide the details.   Exhibit I.
If none, check here: [ ]Yes [ ]No

11. Do you or your spouse or any member of your household, or anyone who owns, manages, or directs your business or their spouses or members of their households work for the Small Business Administration, Small Business Advisory Council, SCORE or ACE, any Federal Agency, or the participating lender? If so, please provide the name and address of the person and the office where employed. Label this Exhibit J.
If none, check here: [ ]

12. Does your business, its owners or majority stockholders own or have a controlling interest in other businesses? If yes, please provide their names and the relationship with your company along with financial data requested in question 4. Label this Exhibit K.

13. Do you buy from, sell to, or use the services of any concern in which someone in your company has a significant financial interest? If yes, provide details on a separate sheet of paper labeled Exhibit L.

14. If your business is a franchise, include a copy of the franchise agreement and a copy of the FTC disclosure statement supplied to you by the Franchisor. Label this Exhibit M.

CONSTRUCTION LOANS ONLY

15. Include as a separate exhibit the estimated cost of the project and a statement of the source of any additional funds. Label this Exhibit N.

16. Provide copies of preliminary construction plans and specifications. Label this as Exhibit 0. Final plans will be required prior to disbursement.

EXPORT LOANS

17. Does your business currently export, or will it start exporting, pursuant to this loan (if approved) ?
Check here: [ ]Yes [ ]No

18. If you answered yes to item 17, what is your estimate of the total export sales this loan would support? $ _____

19. Would you like information on Exporting?
Check here: [ ]Yes [ ]No

COUNSELING/TRAINING

20. Have you received counseling or training from SBA (e.g., SCORE, ACE, SBDC, WBC, etc.) ?
Check here: [ ]Yes [ ]No

AGREEMENTS AND CERTIFICATIONS

Agreements of non-employment of SBA Personnel: I agree that if SBA approves this loan application I will not, for at least two years, hire as an employee or consultant anyone that was employed by the SBA during the one year period prior to the disbursement of the loan.

Certification: I certify:

(a) I have not paid anyone connected with the Federal Government for help in getting this loan. I also agree to report to the SBA office of the Inspector General, Washington, DC 20416 any Federal Government employee who offers, in return for any type of compensation, to help get this loan approved.

(b) All information in this application and the Exhibits are true and complete to the best of my knowledge and are submitted to SBA so SBA can decide whether to grant a loan or participate with a lending institution in a loan to me. I agree to pay for or reimburse SBA for the cost of any surveys, title or mortgage examinations, appraisals, credit reports, etc., performed by non-SBA personnel provided I have given my consent-

(c) I understand that I need not pay anybody to deal with SBA. I have read and understand SBA Form 159 which explains SBA policy on Agents and their fees and have submitted an SBA Form 159 completed by the Agent and myself for each fee covered by SBA Form 159.

(d) As consideration for any Management, Technical, and Business Development Assistance that may be provided, I waive all claims against SBA and its consultants.

(e) I authorize the SBA's Office of Inspector General to request criminal record information about me from criminal justice agencies for the purpose of determining my eligibility for programs authorized by the Small Business Act, as amended.

If you knowingly make a false statement or overvalue a security to obtain a guaranteed loan from SBA, you can be fined up to $10,000 and/or imprisoned for not more than five years under 18 USC 1001; if submitted to a Federally insured institution, under 18 USC 1014 by Imprisonment of not more than twenty years and/or a fine of not more than $1,000,000

If Applicant is a proprietor or general partner, sign below.

By: _____

If Applicant is a Corporation, sign below:

_____
Corporate Name and Seal   Date

By: _____
          Signature of President

Attested by: _____
                Signature of Corporate Secretary

SUBMIT COMPLETED APPLICATION TO LENDER OF CHOICE.

APPLICANT'S CERTIFICATION

By my signature, I certify that I have read and received a copy of the "STATEMENTS REQUIRED BY LAW AND EXECUTIVE ORDER" which was attached to this application. My signature represents my agreement to comply with the approval of my loan request and to comply, whenever applicable, with the hazard insurance, lead-based paint, civil rights or other limitations in this notice.

Each Proprietor, each General Partner, each Limited Partner or Stockholder owning 20% or more, each Guarantor, and the spouse, when applicable, of each of these must sign. Each person should sign only once.

Business Name: _____

By: _____   _____
Signature and Title   Date

Guarantors:

_____   _____
Signature and Title   Date

_____   _____
Signature and Title   Date

_____   _____
Signature and Title   Date

_____   _____
Signature and Title   Date

_____   _____
Signature and Title   Date

_____   _____
Signature and Title   Date

_____   _____
Signature and Title   Date

SBA Form 4 (2-05) Previous Edition Obsolete

Page 4

PLEASE READ, DETACH, AND RETAIN FOR YOUR RECORDS
STATEMENTS REQUIRED BY LAW AND EXECUTIVE ORDER

Federal executive agencies, including the Small Business Administration (SBA), are required to withhold or limit financial assistance, to impose special conditions on approved loans, to provide special notices to applicants or borrowers and to require special reports and data from borrowers in order to comply with legislation passed by the Congress and Executive Orders issued by the President and by the provisions of various inter-agency agreements. SBA has issued regulations and procedures that implement these laws and executive orders, and they are contained in Parts 112, 113, 116, and 117, Title 13, Code of Federal Regulations Chapter 1, or Standard Operating Procedures.

Freedom of Information Act (5 U.S.C. 552)
This law provides, with some exceptions, that SBA must supply information reflected in agency files and records to a person requesting it. Information about approved loans that will be automatically released includes, among other things, statistics on our loan programs (individual borrowers are not identified in the statistics) and other information such as the names of the borrowers (and their officers, directors, stockholders or partners), the collateral pledged to secure the loan, the amount of the loan, its purpose in general terms and the maturity. Proprietary data on a borrower would not routinely be made available to third parties. All requests under this Act are to be addressed to the nearest SBA office and be identified as a Freedom of Information request.

Privacy Act (5 U.S.C. 552a)

A person can request to see or get copies of any personal information that SBA has in his or her file when that file is retrievable by individual identifiers such as name or social security numbers. Requests for information about another party may be denied unless SBA has the written permission of the individual to release the information to the requestor or unless the information is subject to disclosure under the Freedom of Information Act.

Under the provisions of the Privacy Act, you are not required to provide your social security number. Failure to provide your social security number may not affect any right, benefit or privilege to which you are entitled. Disclosures of name and other personal identifiers are, however, required for a benefit, as SBA requires an individual seeking assistance from SBA to provide it with sufficient information for it to make a character determination. In determining whether an individual is of good character, SBA considers the person's integrity, candor, and disposition toward criminal actions. In making loans pursuant to section 7(a)(6) of the Small Business Act (the Act), 15 USC Section 636(a)(6), SBA is required to have reasonable assurance that the loan is of sound value and will be repaid or that it is in the best interest of the Government to grant the assistance requested. Additionally, SBA is specifically authorized to verify your criminal history, or lack thereof, pursuant to section 7(a)(1)(B), 15 USC Section 636(a)(1)(B). Further, for all forms of assistance, SBA is authorized to make all investigations necessary to ensure that a person has not engaged in acts that violate or will violate the Act or the Small Business Investment Act, 15 USC Sections 634(b)(11) and 687(b)(a). For these purposes, you are asked to voluntarily provide your social security number to assist SBA in making a character determination and to distinguish you from other individuals with the same or similar name or other personal identifier.

The Privacy Act authorizes SBA to make certain "routine uses" of information protected by that Act. One such routine use for SBA's loan system of records is that when this information indicates a violation or potential violation of law, whether civil, criminal, or administrative in nature, SBA may refer it to the appropriate agency, whether Federal, State, local or foreign, charged with responsibility for or otherwise involved in investigation, prosecution, enforcement or prevention of such violations. Another routine use of personal information is to assist in obtaining credit bureau reports, including business credit reports on the small business borrower and consumer credit reports and scores on the principals of the small business and guarantors on the loan for purposes of originating, servicing, and liquidating small business loans and for purposes of routine periodic loan portfolio management and lender monitoring. See, 69 F.R. 58598, 58617 (and as amended from time to time) for additional background and other routine uses.

Right to Financial Privacy Act of 1978 (12 U.S.C. 3401)
This is notice to you as required by the Right of Financial Privacy Act of 1978, of SBA's access rights to financial records held by financial institutions that are or have been doing business with you or your business, including any financial institutions participating in a loan or loan guarantee. The law provides that SBA shall have a right of access to your financial records in connection with its consideration or administration of assistance to you in the form of a Government loan or loan guaranty agreement. SBA is required to provide a certificate of its compliance with the Act to a financial institution in connection with its first request for access to your financial records, after which no further certification is required for subsequent accesses. The law also provides that SBA's access rights continue for the term of any approved loan or loan guaranty agreement. No further notice to you of SBA's access rights is required during the term of any such agreement.

The law also authorizes SBA to transfer to another Government authority any financial records included in an application for a loan, or concerning an approved loan or loan guarantee, as necessary to process, service or foreclose on a loan or loan guarantee or to collect on a defaulted loan or loan guarantee. No other transfer of your financial records to another Government authority will be permitted by SBA except as required or permitted by law.

Flood Disaster Protection Act (42 U.S.C. 4011)
Regulations have been issued by the Federal Insurance Administration (FIA) and by SBA implementing this Act and its amendments. These regulations prohibit SBA from making certain loans in an FIA designated floodplain unless Federal flood insurance is purchased as a condition of the loan. Failure to maintain the required level of flood insurance makes the applicant ineligible for any future financial assistance from SBA under any program, including disaster assistance.

Executive Orders -- Floodplain Management and Wetland Protection (42 F.R. 26951 and 42 F.R. 26961)
The SBA discourages any settlement in or development of a floodplain or a wetland. This statement is to notify all SBA loan applicants that such actions are hazardous to both life and property and should be avoided. The additional cost of flood preventive construction must be considered in addition to the possible loss of all assets and investments in future floods.

Occupational Safety and Health Act (15 U.S.C. 651 et seq.)
This legislation authorizes the Occupational Safety and Health Administration in the Department of Labor to require businesses to modify facilities and procedures to protect employees or pay penalty fees. In some instances the business can be forced to cease operations or be prevented from starting operations in a new facility. Therefore, in some instances SBA may require additional information from an applicant to determine whether the business will be in compliance with OSHA regulations and allowed to operate its facility after the loan is approved and disbursed. Signing this form as borrower is a certification that the OSA requirements that apply to the borrower's business have been determined and the borrower to the best of its knowledge is in compliance.

Civil Rights Legislation
All businesses receiving SBA financial assistance must agree not to discriminate in any business practice, including employment practices and services to the public, on the basis of categories cited in 13 C.F.R., Parts 112, 113, and 117 of SBA Regulations. This includes making their goods and services available to handicapped clients or customers. All business borrowers will be required to display the "Equal Employment Opportunity Poster" prescribed by SBA.

Equal Credit Opportunity Act (15 U.S.C. 1691)
The Federal Equal Credit Opportunity Act prohibits creditors from discriminating against credit applicants on the basis of race, color, religion, national origin, sex, marital status or age (provided that the applicant has the capacity to enter into a binding contract); because all or part of the applicant's income derives from any public assistance program, or because the applicant has in good faith exercised any right under the Consumer Credit Protection Act. The Federal agency that administers compliance with this law concerning this creditor is the Federal Trade Commission, Equal Credit Opportunity, Washington, D.C. 20580.

Executive Order 11738 -- Environmental Protection (38 C.F.R. 25161)
The Executive Order charges SBA with administering its loan programs in a manner that will result in effective enforcement of the Clean Air Act, the Federal Water Pollution Act and other environmental protection legislation. SBA must, therefore, impose conditions on some loans. By acknowledging receipt of this form and presenting the application, the principals of all small businesses borrowing $100,000 or more in direct funds stipulate to the following:

1. That any facility used, or to be used, by the subject firm is not cited on the EPA list of Violating Facilities.

2. That subject firm will comply with all the requirements of Section 114 of the Clean Air Act (42 U.S.C. 7414) and Section 308 of the Water Act (33 U.S.C 1318) relating to inspection, monitoring, entry, reports and information, as well as all other requirements specified in Section 114 and Section 308 of the respective Acts, and all regulations and guidelines issued thereunder.

3. That subject firm will notify SBA of the receipt of any communication from the Director of the Environmental Protection Agency indicating that a facility utilized, or to be utilized, by subject firm is under consideration to be listed on the EPA List of Violating Facilities.

Debt Collection Act of 1982 Deficit Reduction Act of 1984 (31 U.S.C. 3701 et seq. and other titles)
These laws require SBA to aggressively collect any loan payments which become delinquent. SBA must obtain your taxpayer identification number when you apply for a loan. If you receive a loan, and do not make payments as they come due, SBA may take one or more of the following actions:

- Report the status of your loan(s) to credit bureaus
- Hire a collection agency to collect your loan
- Offset your income tax refund or other amounts due to you from the Federal Government
- Suspend or debar you or your company from doing business with the Federal Government
- Refer your loan to the Department of Justice or other attorneys for litigation
- Foreclose on collateral or take other action permitted in the loan instruments.

Immigration Reform and Control Act of 1986 (Pub. L. 99-603)
If you are an alien who was in this country illegally since before January 1, 1982, you may have been granted lawful temporary resident status by the United States Immigration and Naturalization Service pursuant to the Immigration Reform and Control Act of 1986 (Pub. L. 99-603). For five years from the date you are granted such status, you are not eligible for financial assistance from the SBA in the form of a loan or guaranty under section 7(a) of the Small Business Act unless you are disabled or a Cuban or Haitian entrant. When you sign this document, you are making the certification that the Immigration Reform and Control Act of 1986 does not apply to you, or if it does apply, more than five years have elapsed since you have been granted lawful temporary resident status pursuant to such 1986 legislation.

Lead-Based Paint Poisoning Prevention Act (42 U.S.C. 4821 et seq.)
Borrowers using SBA funds for the construction or rehabilitation of a residential structure are prohibited from using lead-based paint (as defined in SBA regulations) on all interior surfaces, whether accessible or not, and exterior surfaces, such as stairs, decks, porches, railings, windows and doors, which are readily accessible to children under 7 years of age. A "residential structure" is any home, apartment, hotel, motel, orphanage, boarding school, dormitory, day care center, extended care facility, college or other school housing, hospital, group practice or community facility and all other residential or institutional structures where persons reside.

Executive Order 12549, Debarment and Suspension (13 C.F.R. 145)

1. The prospective lower tier participant certifies, by submission of this loan application, that neither it nor its principals are presently debarred, suspended, proposed for debarment, declared ineligible, or voluntarily excluded from participation in this transaction by any Federal department or agency.

2. Where the prospective lower tier participant is unable to certify to any of the statements in this certification, such prospective participants shall attach an explanation to the loan application.

APPENDIX 17:
STATE WEBSITES FOR BUSINESS
LICENSE INFORMATION

STATE	WEBSITE
Alabama	http://www.ador.state.al.us/licenses/authrity.html
Alaska	http://www.dced.state.ak.us/occ/buslic.htm
Arizona	http://www.revenue.state.az.us/license.htm
Arkansas	http://www.arkansas.gov/business_res.php
California	http://www.calgold.ca.gov/
Colorado	http://www.state.co.us/oed/industry-license/index.cfm
Connecticut	http://www.state.ct.us/
Delaware	http://www.state.de.us/revenue/services/Business_Tax/Step3.shtml
District of Columbia	http://www.dcra.dc.gov/
Florida	http://sun6.dms.state.fl.us/dor/businesses/
Georgia	http://www.sos.state.ga.us/corporations/regforms.htm
Hawaii	http://www.hawaii.gov/dbedt/business/start_grow/
Idaho	http://www.idoc.state.id.us/Pages/BUSINESSPAGE.html
Illinois	http://www.business.illinois.gov/licenses.cfm
Indiana	http://www.state.in.us/sic/owners/ia.html
Iowa	nging.com/business/blic.html /
Kansas	https://www.accesskansas.org/businesscenter/index.html?link=maintain#licenserenewals

STATE	WEBSITE
Kentucky	http://www.thinkkentucky.com/kyedc/ebpermits.asp
Louisiana	http://www.louisiana.gov/wps/portal/.cmd/cs/.ce/155/.s/11 14/_s.155/1110/_me/1110
Maine	http://www.maine.gov/portal/business/licensing.html
Maryland	http://www.dllr.state.md.us/
Massachusetts	http://www.state.ma.us/sec/cor/coridx.htm
Michigan	http://medc.michigan.org/services/startups/index2.asp
Minnesota	http://www.dted.state.mn.uss
Mississippi	http://www.olemiss.edu/depts/mssbdc/going_intobus.html
Missouri	http://www.missouribusiness.net/docs/license_registration _checklist.asp
Montana	http://www.state.mt.us/sos/biz.htm
Nebraska	http://assist.neded.org/licensed.html at this time
New Hampshire	http://www.nhsbdc.org/startup.htm
New Jersey	http://www.state.nj.us/njbiz/s_lic_and_cert.shtml
New York	http://www.dos.state.ny.us/lcns/licensing.html
New Mexico	Not available at this time
Nevada	http://secretaryofstate.biz/comm_rec/index.htm
North Carolina	http://www.secstate.state.nc.us/secstate/blio/default.htm
North Dakota	http://www.nd.gov/sos/businessserv/registrations/business -search.html
Ohio	http://www.sos.state.oh.us/sos/businessservices/corp.aspx
Oklahoma	http://www.okonestop.com/
Oregon	http://www.filinginoregon.com
Pennsylvania	http://www.paopenforbusiness.state.pa.us
Rhode Island	http://www.dlt.ri.gov/lmi/jobseeker/license.htm
South Carolina	http://www.state.sd.us/STATE/sitecategory.cfm?mp= Licenses/Occupations
South Dakota	http://www.sdreadytowork.com/community/resources/ startup/step8.asp

STATE	WEBSITE
Tennessee	http://www.tennesseeanytime.org/business/index.html
Texas	http://www.tded.state.tx.us/guide/
Utah	http://www.commerce.state.ut.us/web/commerce/admin/ licen.htm
Vermont	http://www.sec.state.vt.us/
Virginia	http://www.dba.state.va.us/licenses/
Washington	http://www.wa.gov/dol/bpd/limsnet.htm
West Virginia	http://www.state.wv.us/taxrev/busreg.html
Wisconsin	http://www.wdfi.org/corporations/forms/
Wyoming	http://soswy.state.wy.us/corporat/corporat.htm

SOURCE: U.S. SMALL BUSINESS ADMINISTRATION

APPENDIX 18:
APPLICATION FOR SALES
AND USE TAX PERMIT

ARKANSAS
Department of Finance and Administration
Sales and Use Tax Section
P. O. Box 1272, Little Rock, AR 72203-1272   (501) 682-7104

FORM **ST-1**

For Office Use

Application for Sales and Use Tax Permit
Applicants must answer **ALL** of the requested information fields in order to receive a permit for business in Arkansas.

Complete form in **BLUE or BLACK ink ONLY**

1.
   Name of Business (DBA)
2.
   Corporate Name or Partnership Name
3.
   Location – Street Address of Business (Not P. O. Box)
4.
   Location – Street Address of Business (if additional space is needed)
5.
   City   ST   Zip Code   County (if in Arkansas)
6.
   Business Location Phone Number   Ext
7.
   Mailing Address (if different from Location Address)
8.
   Mailing Address (if additional space is needed)
9.
   City   ST   Zip Code
10.
   Owner/Home Office Phone Number   Ext
11.
   Federal ID
12.
   Name of Owner/Officer or Partner   First   MI   Last

   Title

   Mailing Address of Owner

   Mailing Address of Owner

   City   ST   Zip Code   SSN

13.
   Name of Owner/Officer or Partner   First   MI   Last

   Title

   Mailing Address of Owner

   Mailing Address of Owner

   City   ST   Zip Code   SSN

14. List exactly the products sold or type of service rendered.

Form ST-1 (R 07/2006)

How to Form a Limited Liability Company

135

APPLICATION FOR SALES AND USE TAX PERMIT

15. What's the dollar value of your inventory? _____

16 What's the dollar value of your fixtures and equipment? _____

17. Date you will begin your business? _____
                                          mm/dd/yyyy

18. Check type of business: Retail [ ]   Wholesale [ ]

CHECK TYPE OF BUSINESS ENTITY:

19. Corporation [ ]   S Corporation [ ]   Individual [ ]   Partnership [ ]
        LLC [ ]   LLP [ ]   Government [ ]

20. Date Arkansas Incorporated? _____
                                     mm/dd/yyyy

21. Please check one: Inside city limits [ ]   Outside city limits [ ]

22. Does this business sell or serve beer? ___ wine? ___ liquor? ___ mixed drinks? ___ Private Club? ___
        If YES, please furnish the ABC number under which you are operating. _____

23. Does this business sell tobacco products? _____

24. Do you operate more than one business in Arkansas? _____ If YES, please list all locations, names, addresses and permit numbers on a separate schedule.

25. Did you purchase the inventory, fixtures or equipment of an established business? _____ If YES, give the name and permit number of the business. (attach bill of sale)

_____   _____
Former business name   Former business permit number

26. Are you leasing the property? _____ If YES, attach a copy of the lease agreement.

27. Do you operate a business in your home? _____ If Yes, attach a copy of your city business license or furnish a statement that this license is not required.

28. If you operate an out-of-state business; do you perform any type of repair or service within the state of Arkansas? _____
        If YES, please list exactly the repair or service performed. _____

Important Information

A)   **A $50.00 FEE IS REQUIRED OF ALL ARKANSAS VENDORS ON A RETAIL OR WHOLESALE BASIS.**
     Out of state vendors that lease property into Arkansas or perform taxable services in Arkansas are required to pay
     the $50 registration fee. Please make check payable to **Department of Finance and Administration.**
B)   The former owner of a business must surrender the permit, and report and pay all taxes due by the business through the transfer date. A lien will attach
     to the stock and fixtures to secure the State of Arkansas for delinquent taxes and is enforceable against purchaser.
C)   **Arkansas Code Annotated 26-52-207** states that the tax liability of the former owner transfers to the new owner when the business is sold. No permit
     will be issued to the new owner until all tax liability is paid.

I DECLARE UNDER PENALTY OF PERJURY, THAT THIS APPLICATION (INCLUDING ANY ACCOMPANYING SCHEDULES) HAS
BEEN EXAMINED BY ME, AND TO THE BEST OF MY KNOWLEDGE AND BELIEF IS A TRUE, CORRECT AND COMPLETE
APPLICATION.

_____   _____   _____
Original Signature of Owner/Partner/Officer   Printed Name of Owner/Partner/Officer   Date

FOR OFFICE USE ONLY - DO NOT WRITE IN THIS SPACE

SALES [ ]   USE [ ]   MD [ ]   LE [ ]   AV [ ]   TEX [ ]   SIC: _____

ACCT: _____   COUNTY CODE: _____   LOC CODE: _____   PREVIOUS ACCT: _____

BONDED: _____   ISSUED BY: _____   DATE: _____   PAID BY: _____
                                                                      cash/check/money order

Form ST-1 (R 07/2006)

State of Arkansas
"The Natural State"
Sales and Use Tax Section
7th & Wolfe Streets/Ledbetter Bldg./P. O. Box 1272/Little Rock, AR 72203-1272/(501) 682-7104

Arkansas Application for Permit Instructions - FORM ST-1

GENERAL INSTRUCTIONS
Please **PRINT or TYPE** all information on this form in blue or black ink. Do not add additional blocks or change this form.

LINE-BY-LINE INSTRUCTIONS.

Line 1.   Insert the name of your business **as shown to the public.**

Line 2.   Insert your corporate name if this business is a corporation, sub chapter S corporation, or LLC.

Line 3.   Insert street address where your business is **physically located.** Not your mailing address. Out of state businesses: If you have an Arkansas location, that address would go here.

Line 4.   If your location address takes two lines, then use this line to complete your address.

Line 5.   Insert your city, state, zip code and county of your business location.

Line 6.   Insert the phone number of the store location listed above.

Line 7.   Insert the mailing address of your business if different than location address.

Line 8.   Additional space if mailing address takes two lines.

Line 9.   Insert city, state and zip code of your mailing address.

Line 10. Insert owner's home phone, if business is a sole proprietorship. Insert corporate (home office) phone if a corporation.

Line 11. Insert your federal ID number if your business has one. If your business does not have a federal ID number, then insert the owner's SSN. **Corporations, legal, partnerships, LLCs and LLPs must have a Federal Identification Number before the permit will be issued.**

Line 12. Insert the owner's name, title (President, Vice-President, etc.), mailing address and SSN on these lines. If a corporation, insert corporate officer information. If a partnership, insert partner information. Round owner percentage off to nearest whole number. (**All owners, partners and officers must be listed.**)

Line 13. Same as line 12
          If you need additional owner/partner/officer spaces, use form ST-1-A

Line 14. List the product(s) you sell or the service that you render. **Please be specific.**

Line 15. Enter the dollar value of inventory. If not known exactly, please estimate.

Line 16. Enter the dollar value of fixtures and equipment. If not known exactly, please estimate.

Form ST-1 (R 07/2006)

Line 17. Insert the date you will begin your business. If the actual date is not known, then estimate a date that you believe you will begin your business. **NOTE: Do not submit this application if more than sixty days prior to opening date.**

Line 18. Mark an "X" in the appropriate box, you may select both boxes. Wholesale means you make <u>no</u> sales to the final consumer, all sales are made to businesses that will resell the product.

Line 19. Mark an "X" in the appropriate box.

Line 20. Insert the date your business was incorporated by the State of Arkansas. If your business is not a corporation, skip this line.

Line 21. Mark an "X" in the appropriate box.

Line 22. Answer the questions with either "Yes" or "No". If yes to any question, furnish the ABC permit information.

Line 23 Answer the question with either "Yes" or "No"

Line 24. If you answer "YES" to this question, you must list all of your businesses, permit numbers and locations on a separate page and attach them to this application.

Line 25 Answer the question with either "Yes" or "No". If you answer yes, you must provide the name and permit number of the person from whom you purchased the business.

Line 26. Answer this question, "YES" or "NO". If you answer Yes, attach the Lease Agreement.

Line 27. Answer this question, "YES" or "NO".If you answer Yes, attach a copy of your city license or the statment from the city.

Line 28. Out of state businesses: Answer this question "YES" or "NO". If "YES", then indicate the type of service or repair work performed. **Please be specific.**

<u>ALL QUESTIONS MUST BE ANSWERED</u> for the application to be accepted.
You must sign and date the application for it to be complete and accepted by the department. The application must have the **original** signature of an owner, partner or officer listed on the application.

NOTE: GROSS RECEIPTS (Sales Tax) APPLICANTS AND OUT OF STATE BUSINESSES PERFORMING TAXABLE SERVICES OR LEASING TANGIBLE PERSONAL PROPERTY INTO ARKANSAS:

ATTACH A CHECK FOR THE **$50.00** NON-REFUNDABLE FEE TO THIS APPLICATION. MAKE CHECKS PAYABLE TO: **Department of Finance and Administration**. FAILURE TO ATTACH THE FEE WILL CAUSE DELAYS IN ISSUING YOUR PERMIT.

Visit our web site for more information about Sales Tax: **www.state.ar.us/salestax**

Form ST-1 (R 07/2006)

APPENDIX 19: APPLICATION FOR EMPLOYER IDENTIFICATION NUMBER (FORM SS-4)

Form **SS-4**	**Application for Employer Identification Number**	OMB No. 1545-0003
(Rev. February 2006)	(For use by employers, corporations, partnerships, trusts, estates, churches, government agencies, Indian tribal entities, certain individuals, and others.)	EIN
Department of the Treasury Internal Revenue Service	► See separate instructions for each line. ► Keep a copy for your records.	

1 Legal name of entity (or individual) for whom the EIN is being requested

Type or print clearly.

2 Trade name of business (if different from name on line 1) | **3** Executor, administrator, trustee, "care of" name

4a Mailing address (room, apt., suite no. and street, or P.O. box) | **5a** Street address (if different) (Do not enter a P.O. box.)

4b City, state, and ZIP code | **5b** City, state, and ZIP code

6 County and state where principal business is located

7a Name of principal officer, general partner, grantor, owner, or trustor | **7b** SSN, ITIN, or EIN

8a Type of entity (check only one box)
☐ Sole proprietor (SSN) _____
☐ Partnership
☐ Corporation (enter form number to be filed) ► _____
☐ Personal service corporation
☐ Church or church-controlled organization
☐ Other nonprofit organization (specify) ► _____
☐ Other (specify) ►

☐ Estate (SSN of decedent) _____
☐ Plan administrator (SSN) _____
☐ Trust (SSN of grantor) _____
☐ National Guard ☐ State/local government
☐ Farmers' cooperative ☐ Federal government/military
☐ REMIC ☐ Indian tribal governments/enterprises
Group Exemption Number (GEN) ► _____

8b If a corporation, name the state or foreign country (if applicable) where incorporated | State | Foreign country

9 Reason for applying (check only one box)
☐ Started new business (specify type) ► _____
☐ Hired employees (Check the box and see line 12.)
☐ Compliance with IRS withholding regulations
☐ Other (specify) ►
☐ Banking purpose (specify purpose) ► _____
☐ Changed type of organization (specify new type) ► _____
☐ Purchased going business
☐ Created a trust (specify type) ► _____
☐ Created a pension plan (specify type) ► _____

10 Date business started or acquired (month, day, year). See instructions. | **11** Closing month of accounting year

12 First date wages or annuities were paid (month, day, year). **Note.** If applicant is a withholding agent, enter date income will first be paid to nonresident alien. (month, day, year) _____ ►

13 Highest number of employees expected in the next 12 months (enter -0- if none). | Agricultural | Household | Other

Do you expect to have $1,000 or less in employment tax liability for the calendar year? ☐ **Yes** ☐ **No.** (If you expect to pay $4,000 or less in wages, you can mark yes.)

14 Check one box that best describes the principal activity of your business. ☐ Health care & social assistance ☐ Wholesale-agent/broker
☐ Construction ☐ Rental & leasing ☐ Transportation & warehousing ☐ Accommodation & food service ☐ Wholesale-other ☐ Retail
☐ Real estate ☐ Manufacturing ☐ Finance & insurance ☐ Other (specify)

15 Indicate principal line of merchandise sold, specific construction work done, products produced, or services provided.

16a Has the applicant ever applied for an employer identification number for this or any other business? _____ ☐ Yes ☐ No
Note. If "Yes," please complete lines 16b and 16c.

16b If you checked "Yes" on line 16a, give applicant's legal name and trade name shown on prior application if different from line 1 or 2 above.
Legal name ► | Trade name ►

16c Approximate date when, and city and state where, the application was filed. Enter previous employer identification number if known.
Approximate date when filed (mo., day, year) | City and state where filed | Previous EIN

Third Party Designee	Complete this section **only** if you want to authorize the named individual to receive the entity's EIN and answer questions about the completion of this form.	
	Designee's name	Designee's telephone number (include area code) ( )
	Address and ZIP code	Designee's fax number (include area code) ( )

Under penalties of perjury, I declare that I have examined this application, and to the best of my knowledge and belief, it is true, correct, and complete. | Applicant's telephone number (include area code) ( )

Name and title (type or print clearly) ► | Applicant's fax number (include area code) ( )

Signature ► | Date ►

For Privacy Act and Paperwork Reduction Act Notice, see separate instructions. | Cat. No. 16055N | Form **SS-4** (Rev. 2-2006)

How to Form a Limited Liability Company

139

Do I Need an EIN?

File Form SS-4 if the applicant entity does not already have an EIN but is required to show an EIN on any return, statement, or other document.[1] See also the separate instructions for each line on Form SS-4.

IF the applicant...	AND...	THEN...
Started a new business	Does not currently have (nor expect to have) employees	Complete lines 1, 2, 4a–8a, 8b (if applicable), and 9–16c.
Hired (or will hire) employees, including household employees	Does not already have an EIN	Complete lines 1, 2, 4a–6, 7a–b (if applicable), 8a, 8b (if applicable), and 9–16c.
Opened a bank account	Needs an EIN for banking purposes only	Complete lines 1–5b, 7a–b (if applicable), 8a, 9, and 16a–c.
Changed type of organization	Either the legal character of the organization or its ownership changed (for example, you incorporate a sole proprietorship or form a partnership)[2]	Complete lines 1–16c (as applicable).
Purchased a going business[3]	Does not already have an EIN	Complete lines 1–16c (as applicable).
Created a trust	The trust is other than a grantor trust or an IRA trust[4]	Complete lines 1–16c (as applicable).
Created a pension plan as a plan administrator[5]	Needs an EIN for reporting purposes	Complete lines 1, 3, 4a–8a, 8a, 9, and 16a–c.
Is a foreign person needing an EIN to comply with IRS withholding regulations	Needs an EIN to complete a Form W-8 (other than Form W-8ECI), avoid withholding on portfolio assets, or claim tax treaty benefits[6]	Complete lines 1–5b, 7a–b (SSN or ITIN optional), 8a–9, and 16a–c.
Is administering an estate	Needs an EIN to report estate income on Form 1041	Complete lines 1, 2, 3, 4a–6, 8a, 9-11, 12-15 (if applicable), and 16a–c.
Is a withholding agent for taxes on non-wage income paid to an alien (i.e., individual, corporation, or partnership, etc.)	Is an agent, broker, fiduciary, manager, tenant, or spouse who is required to file Form 1042, Annual Withholding Tax Return for U.S. Source Income of Foreign Persons	Complete lines 1, 2, 3 (if applicable), 4a–5b, 7a–b (if applicable), 8a, 9, and 16a–c.
Is a state or local agency	Serves as a tax reporting agent for public assistance recipients under Rev. Proc. 80-4, 1980-1 C.B. 581[7]	Complete lines 1, 2, 4a–5b, 8a, 9, and 16a–c.
Is a single-member LLC	Needs an EIN to file Form 8832, Entity Classification Election, for filing employment tax returns, or for state reporting purposes[8]	Complete lines 1–16c (as applicable).
Is an S corporation	Needs an EIN to file Form 2553, Election by a Small Business Corporation[9]	Complete lines 1–16c (as applicable).

[1] For example, a sole proprietor or self-employed farmer who establishes a qualified retirement plan, or is required to file excise, employment, alcohol, tobacco, or firearms returns, must have an EIN. A partnership, corporation, REMIC (real estate mortgage investment conduit), nonprofit organization (church, club, etc.), or farmers' cooperative must use an EIN for any tax-related purpose even if the entity does not have employees.

[2] However, do not apply for a new EIN if the existing entity only (a) changed its business name, (b) elected on Form 8832 to change the way it is taxed (or is covered by the default rules), or (c) terminated its partnership status because at least 50% of the total interests in partnership capital and profits were sold or exchanged within a 12-month period. The EIN of the terminated partnership should continue to be used. See Regulations section 301.6109-1(d)(2)(iii).

[3] Do not use the EIN of the prior business unless you became the "owner" of a corporation by acquiring its stock.

[4] A plan administrator is the person or group of persons specified as the administrator by the instrument under which the plan is operated.

[5] A plan administrator is the person or group of persons specified as the administrator by the instrument under which the plan is operated.

[6] Entities applying to be a Qualified Intermediary (QI) need a QI-EIN even if they already have an EIN. See Rev. Proc. 2000-12.

[7] See also Household employer on page 3. Note. State or local agencies may need an EIN for other reasons, for example, hired employees.

[8] Most LLCs do not need to file Form 8832. See Limited liability company (LLC) on page 4 for details on completing Form SS-4 for an LLC.

[9] An existing corporation that is electing or revoking S corporation status should use its previously-assigned EIN.

How to Form a Limited Liability Company

APPENDIX 20:
ARTICLES OF DISSOLUTION—
DOMESTIC LLC

New York State
Department of State
Division of Corporations, State Records
and Uniform Commercial Code
Albany, NY 12231
www.dos.state.ny.us

ARTICLES OF DISSOLUTION
OF

_____
(Insert name of Domestic Limited Liability Company)

Under Section 705 of the Limited Liability Company Law

FIRST: The name of the limited liability company is: _____

If the name of the limited liability company has been changed, the name under which it was organized is: _____.

SECOND: The articles of organization were filed with the Department of State on

THIRD: The event giving rise to the filing of the articles of dissolution is (*check the appropriate statement*):

_____ The vote or written consent of a majority in interest of the members of the limited liability company.

There are no members of the limited liability company.

_____ Pursuant to the dissolution date set forth in the articles of organization or operating agreement of the limited liability company.

X_____
(Signature)

_____
(Type or print name)

_____
(Title of signer)

ARTICLES OF DISSOLUTION
OF

(Insert name of Domestic Limited Liability Company)
Under Section 705 of the Limited Liability Company Law

Filed by:
(Name)

(Mailing address)

(City, State and Zip code)

NOTE: This form was prepared by the New York State Department of State for filing a certificate of dissolution for a domestic limited liability company. It does not contain all optional provisions under the law. You are not required to use this form. You may draft your own form or use forms available at legal supply stores. The Department of State recommends that legal documents be prepared under the guidance of an attorney. The certificate must be submitted with a $60 filing fee made payable to the Department of State.

(For office use only.)

GLOSSARY

ACCOUNTS PAYABLE—Trade accounts of businesses representing obligations to pay for goods and services received.

ACCOUNTS RECEIVABLE—Trade accounts of businesses representing monies due for goods sold or services rendered evidenced by notes, statements, invoices or other written evidence of a present obligation.

ACCOUNTING—The recording, classifying, summarizing and interpreting in a significant manner and in terms of money, transactions and events of a financial character.

AGENCY—The relationship between a principal and an agent who is employed by the principal, to perform certain acts dealing with third parties.

AGENT—One who represents another known as the principal.

APPARENT AGENCY—Apparent agency exists when one person, whether or not authorized, reasonably appears to a third person to be authorized to act as agent for such other.

ASSUMPTION—The act of assuming/undertaking another's debts or obligations.

AUCTION—A public sale of goods to the highest bidder.

AUTOMATIC DATA PROCESSING—Data processing largely performed by automatic means.

BALANCE SHEET—A report of the status of a firm's assets, liabilities and owner's equity at a given time.

BAD FAITH—A willful failure to comply with one's statutory or contractual obligations.

BANKRUPTCY—A condition in which a business cannot meet its debt obligations and petitions a federal district court for either reorganization of its debts or liquidation of its assets.

BOARD OF DIRECTORS—The governing body of a corporation which is elected by the stockholders.

BOILERPLATE—Refers to standard language found almost universally in certain documents.

BREAK-EVEN POINT—The break-even point in any business is that point at which the volume of sales or revenues exactly equals total expenses—i.e., the point at which there is neither a profit nor loss.

BUSINESS BIRTH—Formation of a new establishment or enterprise.

BUSINESS DEATH—Voluntary or involuntary closure of a firm or establishment.

BUSINESS DISSOLUTION—For enumeration purposes, the absence from any current record of a business that was present in a prior time period.

BUSINESS FAILURE—The closure of a business causing a loss to at least one creditor.

BUSINESS INFORMATION CENTER (BIC)—One of more than 50 specialized Small Business Administration units which offer the latest in high-technology hard-ware, software and telecommunications to assist small business and one-on-one counseling with seasoned business veterans through the Service Corps of Retired Executives (SCORE).

BUSINESS PLAN—A comprehensive planning document which clearly describes the business developmental objective of an existing or proposed business and outlines what and how and from where the resources needed to accomplish the objective will be obtained and utilized.

BUSINESS START—For enumeration purposes, a business with a name or similar designation that did not exist in a prior time period.

CANCELED LOAN—The annulment or rescission of an approved loan prior to disbursement.

CAPITAL—Assets less liabilities, representing the ownership interest in a business.

CAPITAL CONTRIBUTION—Cash, property or services contributed by partners to a partnership.

CAPITAL EXPENDITURES—Business spending on additional equipment and inventory.

CAPITAL GAIN—The excess of proceeds over cost, or other basis, from the sale of a capital asset.

CAPITAL LOSS—Loss on the sale or exchange of a capital asset.

CAPITALIZED PROPERTY—Personal property of the business which has an average dollar value of $300.00 or more and a life expectancy of one year or more.

CASH FLOW—The amount of funds a business receives during any given period minus what is paid out during the same period.

CENTRALIZATION OF MANAGEMENT—An organization has centralized management if any person—or any group of persons which does not include all of the members of the organization—has continuing exclusive authority to make the management decisions necessary to the conduct of the business for which the organization was formed.

CHARTER—The document issued by the government establishing a corporate entity.

CLOSE CORPORATION—A corporation whose shares, or at least voting shares, are held by a single shareholder or closely-knit group of shareholders.

CLOSED LOAN—Any loan for which funds have been disbursed, and all required documentation has been executed, received and reviewed.

CLOSING—Actions and procedures required to effect the documentation and disbursement of loan funds after the application has been approved, and the execution of all required documentation and its filing and recordation where required.

COLLATERAL—Something of value—securities, evidence of deposit or other property—pledged to support the repayment of an obligation.

COLLATERAL DOCUMENT—A legal document covering the item(s) pledged as collateral on a loan, e.g., note, mortgages, assignment, etc.

COMMINGLE—To combine funds or properties into a common fund.

COMPROMISE—The settlement of a claim resulting from a defaulted loan for less than the full amount due.

CONSOLIDATION—A combination of two or more corporations which are succeeded by a new corporation, usually with a new title.

CONSORTIUM—A coalition of organizations, such as banks and corporations, set up to fund ventures requiring large capital resources.

CONSUMER CREDIT—Loans and sale credit extended to individuals to finance the purchases of goods and services arising out of consumer needs and desires.

CONTINGENT LIABILITY—A potential obligation that may be incurred dependent upon the occurrence of a future event.

CONTINUITY OF LIFE—An organization has continuity of life if the death, insanity, bankruptcy, retirement, resignation, or expulsion of any member will not cause a dissolution of the organization.

CONTRACT—A contract is an agreement between two or more persons which creates an obligation to do or not to do a particular thing.

CORPORATION—A group of persons granted a state charter legally recognizing them as a separate entity having its own rights, privileges, and liabilities distinct from those of its members.

COSTS—Money obligated for goods and services received during a given period of time, regardless of when ordered or whether paid for.

DEBT CAPITAL—Business financing that normally requires periodic interest payments and repayment of the principal within a specified time.

DEBT FINANCING—The provision of long-term loans to small business concerns in exchange for debt securities or a note.

DEFAULTS—The nonpayment of principal and/or interest on the due date as provided by the terms and conditions of the note.

DEFERRED LOAN—Loans whose principal and or interest installments are postponed for a specified period of time.

DIVESTITURE—Change of ownership and/or control of a business from a majority to disadvantaged persons.

DOMESTIC CORPORATION—In reference to a particular state, a domestic corporation is one created by, or organized under, the laws of that state.

EARNING POWER—The demonstrated ability of a business to earn a profit, over time, while following good accounting practices.

ENTERPRISE—Aggregation of all establishments owned by a parent company, which may consist of a single, independent establishment or subsidiaries or other branch establishments under the same ownership and control.

ENTREPRENEUR—One who assumes the financial risk of the initiation, operation and management of a given business or undertaking.

EQUITY—An ownership interest in a business.

EQUITY FINANCING—The provision of funds for capital or operating expenses in exchange for capital stock, stock purchase warrants and options in the business financed, without any guaranteed return, but with the opportunity to share in the company's profits.

EQUITY PARTNERSHIP—A limited partnership arrangement for providing start-up and seed capital to businesses.

ESTABLISHMENT—A single-location business unit, which may be independent—called a single-establishment enterprise—or owned by a parent enterprise.

FEDERAL TRADE COMMISSION—The Federal Trade Commission is an agency of the federal government created in 1914 for the purpose of promoting free and fair competition in interstate commerce through the prevention of general trade restraints.

FINANCE CHARGE—Any charge for an extension of credit, such as interest.

FINANCIAL REPORTS—Reports commonly required from applicants who request financial assistance such as balance sheets, income statements and cash flow charts.

FINANCING—New funds provided to a business, by either loans or purchase of debt securities or capital stock.

FISCAL YEAR—Any twelve-month period used by a business as its fiscal accounting period.

FIXED CAPITAL—The amount of money permanently invested in a business.

FLOW CHART—A graphical representation for the definition, analysis, or solution of a problem, in which symbols are used to represent operations, data, flow, equipment, etc.

FOREIGN CORPORATION—In reference to a particular state, a foreign corporation is one created by or under the laws of another state, government or country.

FRANCHISING—A form of business by which the owner—i.e., the franchisor—of a product, service or method obtains distribution through affiliated dealers—i.e., the franchisees—and whereby the product, method or service being marketed is usually identified by the franchisor's brand name, and the franchisee is often given exclusive access to a defined geographical area as well as assistance in organizing, training, merchandising, marketing and managing in return for a consideration.

FREE TRANSFERABILITY OF INTERESTS—An organization is considered to have the characteristic of free transferability of interests if each of its members, or those members owning substantially all of the interests in the organization, have the power to substitute for themselves in the organization a person who is not otherwise a member, without the consent of the other members.

GENERAL PARTNER—A partner who participates fully in the profits, losses and management of the partnership, and who is personally liable for its debts.

GENERAL PARTNERSHIP—A type of partnership in which all of the partners share the profits and losses as well as the management fully, though their capital contributions may vary.

GROSS DOMESTIC PRODUCT (GDP)—The most comprehensive single measure of aggregate economic output representing the market value of the total output of the goods and services produced by a nation's economy.

GUARANTEED LOAN—A loan made and serviced by a lending institution under agreement that a governmental agency will purchase the guaranteed portion if the borrower defaults.

HAZARD INSURANCE—Insurance required showing lender as loss payee covering certain risks on real and personal property used for securing loans.

IMPOSSIBILITY—Impossibility is a defense to breach of contract and arises when performance is impossible due to the destruction of the subject matter of the contract or the death of a person necessary for performance.

INCOME STATEMENT—A report of revenue and expenses which shows the results of business operations or net income for a specified period of time.

INCORPORATION—To form a corporation by following established legal procedures.

INDEMNIFICATION CLAUSE—An indemnification clause in a contract refers to the agreement by one party to secure the other party against loss or damage which may occur in the future in connection with performance of the contract.

INDEMNIFY—To hold another harmless for loss or damage which has already occurred, or which may occur in the future.

INNOVATION—Introduction of a new idea into the marketplace in the form of a new product or service, or an improvement in organization or process.

INSOLVENCY—The inability of a borrower to meet financial obligations as they mature, or having insufficient assets to pay legal debts.

INTEREST—An amount paid a lender for the use of funds.

INVESTMENT BANKING—Businesses specializing in the formation of capital.

JOB DESCRIPTION—A written statement listing the elements of a particular job or occupation, e.g., purpose, duties, equipment used, qualifications, training, physical and mental demands, working conditions, etc.

JUDGMENT—Judicial determination of the existence of an indebtedness, or other legal liability.

JUDGMENT BY CONFESSION—The act of debtors permitting judgment to be entered against them for a given sum with a statement to that effect, without the institution of legal proceedings.

JUDGMENT CREDITOR—A creditor who has obtained a judgment against a debtor, which judgment may be enforced to obtain payment of the amount due.

JUDGMENT DEBTOR—An individual who owes a sum of money, and against whom a judgment has been awarded for that debt.

JUNK BOND—A high-yield corporate bond issue with a below-investment rating that became a growing source of corporate funding in the 1980s.

LEASE—A contract between an owner—i.e., a lessor—and a tenant—i.e., a lessee—stating the conditions under which the tenant may occupy or use the property.

LEGAL RATE OF INTEREST—The maximum rate of interest fixed by the laws of the various states, which a lender may charge a borrower for the use of money.

LENDING INSTITUTION—Any institution, including a commercial bank, savings and loan association, commercial finance company, or other lender qualified to participate in the making of loans.

LETTER OF INTENT- A non-binding writing intended to set forth the intentions between parties in anticipation of a formal, binding contract.

LEVERAGED BUY-OUT—The purchase of a business, with financing provided largely by borrowed money, often in the form of junk bonds.

LIEN—A charge upon or security interest in real or personal property maintained to ensure the satisfaction of a debt or duty ordinarily arising by operation of law.

LIMITED LIABILITY—An organization has the characteristic of limited liability if under local law there is no member who is personally liable for the organization's debts.

LIMITED LIABILITY COMPANY (LLC)—A hybrid business formation with certain advantageous features of both a partnership (e.g. pass through income) and a corporation (e.g., limited liability).

LIMITED PARTNER—A partner whose participation in the profits of the business is limited by agreement and who is not liable for the debts of the partnership beyond his or her capital contribution.

LIMITED PARTNERSHIP—A type of partnership comprised of one or more general partners who manage the business and who are personally liable for partnership debts, and one or more limited partners who contribute capital and share in profits but who take no part in running the business and incur no liability with respect to partnership obligations beyond contribution.

LINE OF CREDIT—An arrangement whereby a financial institution commits itself to lend up to a specified maximum amount of funds during a specified period.

LIQUIDATION—The disposal, at maximum prices, of the collateral securing a loan, and the voluntary and enforced collection of the remaining loan balance from the obligators and/or guarantors.

LIQUIDATION VALUE—The net value realizable in the sale—ordinarily a forced sale—of a business or a particular asset.

LITIGATION—The practice of taking legal action through the judicial process.

LOAN AGREEMENT—Agreement to be executed by borrower, containing pertinent terms, conditions, covenants and restrictions.

LOAN PAYOFF AMOUNT—The total amount of money needed to meet a borrower's obligation on a loan.

LOSS RATE—A rate developed by comparing the ratio of total loans charged off to the total loans disbursed from inception of the program to the present date.

MARKET—The set of existing and prospective users of a product or service.

MARKET PENETRATION—A systematic campaign to increase sales in current markets of an existing product or service.

MARKET SEGMENT—A distinct or definable subset of a target market.

MERGER—A combination of two or more corporations wherein the dominant unit absorbs the passive ones, and the former continuing operation usually under the same name.

NET ASSETS—Total assets minus total liabilities.

NET INCOME—The excess of all revenues and gains for a period over all expenses and losses of the same period.

NET LOSS—The excess of all expenses and losses for a period over all revenues and gains of the same period.

NET WORTH—Property owned, i.e.—assets—minus debts and obligations owed—i.e., liabilities—is the owner's net worth—i.e., equity.

NOTES AND ACCOUNTS RECEIVABLE—A secured or unsecured receivable evidenced by a note or open account arising from activities involving liquidation and disposal of loan collateral.

ORGANIZATIONAL CHART—A linear direction of responsibility and authority within a company or institution.

OUTLAYS—Net disbursements for administrative expenses and for loans and related costs and expenses.

PARTNERSHIP—A legal relationship existing between two or more persons contractually associated as joint principals in a business.

PATENT—A patent secures the exclusive right to make, use and sell an invention for 17 years.

PIERCING THE CORPORATE VEIL—The process of holding another liable, such as an individual, for the acts of a corporation.

PRIME RATE—Interest rate which is charged business borrowers having the highest credit ratings, for short-term borrowing.

PRODUCT LIABILITY—Type of tort or civil liability that applies to product manufacturers and sellers.

PROFESSIONAL ASSOCIATIONS—Non-profit, cooperative and voluntary organizations that are designed to help their members in dealing with problems of mutual interest.

PROFESSIONAL MALPRACTICE—The failure of one rendering professional services to exercise that degree of skill and learning commonly applied in the community by the average prudent reputable member of the profession, with the result of injury, loss or damage to the recipient of those services, or to those entitled to rely upon them.

PROFIT—Excess of revenues over expenses for a transaction.

PROFIT AND LOSS STATEMENT—Statement of income.

PROFIT MARGIN—Sales minus all expenses.

PROPRIETORSHIP—The most common legal form of business ownership comprising about 85 percent of all small businesses and whereby the liability of the owner is unlimited.

PRO-RATA BASIS—Proportionately.

PROSPECTUS—A document given by a company to prospective investors, which sets forth all the material information concerning the company and its financial stability, so the investor can make an informed decision on whether to invest in it.

RATIO—Denotes relationships of items within and between financial statements, e.g., current ratio, quick ratio, inventory turnover ratio and debt/net worth ratios.

RETURN ON INVESTMENT—The amount of profit—i.e., return—based on the amount of resources—i.e., funds—used to produce it.

SCOPE OF EMPLOYMENT—Those activities performed while carrying out the business of one's employer.

SERVICE CORPS OF RETIRED EXECUTIVES (SCORE)—Retired, and working, successful business persons who volunteer to render assistance in counseling, training and guiding small business clients.

SHAREHOLDER—A person who owns shares of stock in a corporation or joint-stock company, also referred to as a stockholder.

SHERMAN ANTITRUST ACT—A federal statute passed in 1890 to prohibit monopolization and unreasonable restraint of trade in interstate and foreign commerce.

SILENT PARTNER—An investor in a business who is either unidentified to third parties, or who does not take an active role in day-to-day management of the business.

SMALL BUSINESS DEVELOPMENT CENTER (SBDC)—The SBDC is a university-based center for the delivery of joint government, academic, and private sector services for the benefit of small business and the national welfare which is committed to the development and productivity of business and the economy in specific geographical regions.

SMALL BUSINESS ADMINISTRATION (SBA)—Organization whose fundamental purpose is to aid, counsel, assists and protect the interest of small businesses.

SMALL BUSINESS CORPORATION—A corporation which satisfies the definition of I.R.C. §1371(a), §1244(c)(2) or both. Satisfaction of I.R.C. §1371(a) permits a Subchapter S election, while satisfaction of I.R.C. §1244 enables the shareholders of the corporation to claim an ordinary loss on the worthlessness of the stock.

SMALL BUSINESS INVESTMENT ACT—Federal legislation enacted in 1958 under which investment companies may be organized for supplying long term equity capital to small businesses.

SOLE PROPRIETORSHIP—A form of business in which one person owns all the assets of the business, and is solely liable for the debts of the business.

STOCK CERTIFICATE—A certificate issued to a shareholder which evidences partial ownership of the shareholder in a company.

TAFT-HARTLEY ACT—Refers to the Labor-Management Relations Act of 1947, which was established to prescribe the legitimate rights of both employees and employers.

TRADE ASSOCIATION—An organization established to benefit members of the same trade by informing them of issues and developments within the organization and about how changes outside the organization will affect them.

TRADE CREDIT—Debt arising through credit sales and recorded as an account receivable by the seller and as an account payable by the buyer.

TRADEMARK—Any word, name, symbol, or device, or any combination thereof used to identify and distinguish one's goods from those manufactured or sold by others and to indicate the source of the goods, even if that source is unknown.

TRADE NAME—Any name used by a person to identify his or her business or vocation; commercial name.

TURNOVER—As it pertains to a business, turnover is the number of times that an average inventory of goods is sold during a fiscal year or some designated period which measures the efficiency of a business.

UNIFORM COMMERCIAL CODE (UCC)—The UCC is a code of laws governing commercial transactions which was designed to bring uniformity to the laws of the various states.

UNION SHOP—A workplace where all of the employees are members of a union.

VENDOR—A seller.

VENTURE CAPITAL—Money used to support new or unusual commercial undertakings; equity, risk or speculative capital.

WORKERS' COMPENSATION—A state-mandated form of insurance covering workers injured in job-related accidents.

WORKING CAPITAL—Current assets minus current liabilities.

ZONE OF EMPLOYMENT—The physical area within which injuries to an employee are covered by worker compensation laws.

BIBLIOGRAPHY AND ADDITIONAL READING

Black's Law Dictionary, Fifth Edition. St. Paul, MN: West Publishing Company, 1979.

CCH Incorporated (Date Visited: May 2007) <http://www.cch.com/>.

Findlaw (Date Visited: May 2007) <http://www.findlaw.com/>.

Internal Revenue Service (Date Visited: May 2007)

Small Business Administration (Date Visited: May 2007) <http://www.sba.gov/>.

Social Security Administration (Date Visited: May 2007) <http://www.ssa.gov/>.

Legal Information Institute (Date Visited: May 2007) <http://www.law.cornell.edu/>.

Nolo Press (Date Visited: May 2007) <http://www.nolo.com/>.

The United States Department of Labor (Date Visited: May 2007) <http://www.dol.gov/>.

The United States Patent and Trademark Office (Date Visited: May 2007) <http:www.uspto.org>.

The United States Security and Exchange Commission (Date Visited: May 2007) <http://www.sec.gov/>.